Cake

....a savvy gal's guide
to the sweet life.

Sherry Wilsher

TAG

TAG Publishing, LLC
2618 S. Lipscomb
Amarillo, TX 79109

www.TAGPublishers.com
Office (806) 373-0114
Fax (806) 373-4004
info@TAGPublishers.com

Quantity discounts are available on bulk orders.
For more information contact: sales@TAGPublishers.com

Cake: A Savvy Gal's Guide to the Sweet Life
First Edition

ISBN: 978-1-934606-31-5

Cover and layout design created by:
Ashlee Lynch
AshleeLynch.com

Cake

....a savvy gal's guide
to the sweet life.

Sherry Wilsher

* *Dedication* **

To My Father:
Gary Allen Richardson, Sr.
1945 - 2007

. . . .

Daddy, may the words of this book express the true essence of the love we have shared - the purest of all forms. Though I miss seeing you daily in physical form, I am connected to you now more than ever before. We are linked in heart and spirit; a stronger bond than any earthly ties.

Thank you for your unending and unconditional love. It is returned in endless measure.

Eternal love,

Sherry

Oh, and P.S. - I appreciate the heads up on Heaven! It all makes perfect sense now.

Following my dreams has taken me down many pathways.
Some have been smooth, others not so smooth.
The expereinces that have been the rockiest have been the
ones I look back on and smile because if not for those
"learning experiences" I would not be the woman I am today.

*About the Author * *

S herry Wilsher is a multifaceted businesswoman who knows how to have her cake and eat it too. After spending a decade in the field of cosmetic dentistry, she launched a successful real estate career, designed, developed and patented her own invention, and recreated her life. The native Texan prides herself on her innovative ideas and unwavering self confidence. Sherry's triumphant victory over divorce and losing everything she worked for inspired her to share her story with the world.

Determination, old world sensibility and Texas tenacity have taught Sherry that anything is possible. The sky's the limit, even in Texas, where everything is bigger. Sherry's recipe for the sweet life derived from her constant pursuit to find the meaning of true happiness. Her life experiences are a testament that everyone can maintain bliss in any situation or circumstance. Sherry currently savors the sweet life in Houston, Texas.

*Come to the Table **

Foreword **

Tina Dezsi
Author, Speaker and CEO/Founder
Power of Women Exchange

*A*s I read the pages of this delightful book, I nod my head with what Sherry so eloquently shares, told in a language every woman can understand.

This book is about a journey, one that we as women today can relate to. We are supposed to have it all: the loving husband, the perfect family, a sparkling clean home, and the occasional trip to paradise. How do we know this? We are taught through experience, from our mothers, the media, and even in our dreams.

We dream of our Prince Charming, who will come along just for us. He will sweep us away to live happily ever after…but wait, STOP the presses! We have seen it all with our mothers, sisters, and girlfriends. How true is that really? Yet when some version of Prince Charming comes along, we run, jump, and trip over our stilettos to make him fit into our ideal.

Sherry relates her own truth in such a perfectly set table that even Miss Manners couldn't find fault. Ah, but the truth is on the inside. She knew some key ingredients to her happiness were missing and she struggled with the conflicting ideas of the good girl she was supposed to be, was brought up to be, and the real woman she was meant to be.

With all the tasty treats that life has to offer her tucked away in the top cupboard in the kitchen, just out of reach. Knowing it's there, but never getting the step stool (her nerve) to have a taste. Fear, anger, and duty kept her from seeking the delicious joy that could be hers.

The 'good girl' in her always prevailed. Her years of learning how to behave, and the desire not to open the oven and allow the cake to fall, were always the most important things.

The story and the recipes in this book are of an emotional journey captured in a smorgasbord of brilliant transformation, written in delightfully tasteful metaphors for life, from the Come to the Table to the Final Food for Thought, Sherry has created a blueprint to enable any woman to trust in her own instincts.

By using all of her past experiences combined with the new recipes in this book, she can set herself up for success by seeking out only the very best of ingredients to produce a successful life within ourselves and then eventually with someone else, but only the right someone.

My hope for you is to find those perfect ingredients ahead of time, combine them with experience, love, thoughtfulness with the deepest care for yourself as you create a delicious life. Using Sherry's recipes for happiness, you are sure to take fewer steps than she has and create a life of self-love and love with someone else with ease and flow.

> *So will I sing praise unto thy name forever, that*
> *I may daily perform my vows.*
> *- Psalm 61:8*

And now these three remain: faith,
hope and love.
But the greatest of these is love.

~ 1 Corinthians 13:13 ~

Introduction

Warming Up the Blissful Life Bakery Oven

*T*hank you for picking up a slice of Cake – It is my hope that you will devour every morsel and gain nourishment, joy, inspiration, and a recipe for your sweetest, most satisfying life. Throughout this book, I'll be talking about creating your best life right now and that life is your own personal journey to happiness, your 'Cake'. This is not about the other people in your life, this is about you and how you can achieve balance and joy, no matter your present circumstances.

You will also notice that I like to frequently say, "frosting is optional". Most all cakes have some sort of frosting, which for many women means a spouse or life partner. These relationships can enhance your life, but they are not vital to live a full and rewarding existence. We'll talk about the frosting a little later.

Of course, I cannot promise that everything will be perfect, but I can promise that if you take this journey with me, you will learn a little about life, spirituality, having it all (not doing it all), and the realization that Cake (your life) is delicious all on its own. The frosting is optional and enhances what you have already created.

I chose the analogy of cake for this book because like life, cake is layered, filled with sugar and spice, and can fall flat if the recipe's not right. Also like life, it takes a mixture of ingredients. The proportions need to be well measured, and one layer should not outweigh another. In other words: Balance. The types and varieties of cake are endless and are a true reflection of the cook, rather than the ingredients. Each individual has the ability to create any kind of cake they choose at any moment and this mirrors our ability to choose the life we want to live at any time.

For many cultures, cake is the ultimate dessert – every cuisine in the world has some form of cake – and while the ingredients vary, the thrill, fun and excitement of making each one unique in its own way is the same around the world. The purpose of this book is to share life experiences that led me to discover the sweet life that I live today. Previously, I possessed a very limited mindset and was unaware how much choice and control I had in my own life. By sharing my own journey, hopefully you will gain some insight to create your own sweet life, especially if your life is currently 'crumby' or you have been settling for leftovers. This book will help you bake a solid, satisfying confection of your life and allow you to live with passion, purpose, and joy.

When I decided to write this book, I initially wanted to talk about my clever patented invention and the creative process I had gone through, from conception to reality. However, after I completed my first draft, something inside didn't feel right. I asked myself, "What do you really want out of life? What would you like to share with readers?"

I pondered these questions and my answer stunned me. For so long, my thoughts swirled around being the head of a successful corporation; I believed that was my dream. To take one of my great ideas to market, make millions, and have many homes around the world. That seemed like a pretty nifty life to me.

That dream lasted until I had a heart to heart talk with myself and found some real truths that have nothing to do with heading a successful company or making millions. No one wants to read how Miss Perfect became the next Donald Trump. What they do want to know is how I got through some of the darkest days of my life and still found the strength to keep going. Isn't that what we all want to know? Of course it is! If it wasn't, Oprah wouldn't have an audience!

It can be hard for anyone to open up and share some of the not so great moments in their life and it's hard for me too. I didn't want to write down some of those hard times, but I realized they are a part of me and those events brought me to the wonderful life I have now. I know I learn the most about myself and what I am capable of when times are hard, not when they are easy and the same is true for many of us.

Today, I am happy in my own skin and for the first time in my life, I love myself for who I was created to be. Not who society thinks I should be, but for who I am and what I hold dear. It is my hope that you too will find this same peace – the peace that is the underlying essence of why we are here. We all have an ultimate purpose and I encourage you to find yours. Once you do, you will never worry about having regrets or wonder if you are missing out. You will be living, really living, perhaps for the first time in your life.

After years of living my life loving, laughing, crying, experimenting, having cake sometimes, going without it at others, I finally realized that my cake lacked the most precious ingredient, true happiness. Not the surface kind of happiness where you get along with family or like your job, but that real deep down happiness that only comes from balance and love of who you are as a person. I look back at photos of myself over the years and I can see the smile on my face but it doesn't quite reach my eyes. I was just trying to keep all the balls in the air – running here, running there, getting through life but not being really happy. How could I have lived so many years this way?

Truth is, I substituted lots of other less ideal ingredients for the happiness quotient; they all failed. I tried settling, shopping, being a workaholic, partying, inventing, dating the wrong guy, marrying for the wrong reasons, and many other ridiculously wrong additives. I'm willing to bet you have too.

One day I realized I promised to bake a birthday cake for a friend's daughter. Alison was going to be seven and requested my strawberry-lemon cake with cream cheese frosting. I baked the cake layers, put them on a rack to cool, and prepared to make the frosting. Then it happened! I tore the refrigerator apart, but alas, there was no cream cheese. None. The party was about to begin; no time to shop. I felt horrible!

I called Alison's mom and confessed.

"Don't worry about it," she said calmly. "Your strawberry cake is delicious! I've always thought the frosting was optional anyway. Just bring the cake, smile, and everything will be fine."

That thought stuck with me for a long time; cake is delicious. Who needs frosting? It is definitely nice, extra sweet, but completely optional.

My life was set on auto pilot and the flight pattern was just a big circle. No matter what I tried to do to create happiness, I ended up back at square one and had the same question:

"Why am I so unhappy?"

With no clear answer, I was off to another temporary distraction to divert my attention long enough to fool myself into thinking I was heading toward my ultimate happiness goal. Problem was, I had no real goal, only the vague destination of "Happiness, U.S.A." To compound my problem, it turns out there is no place named Happiness, because life is all about the journey, not the destination. I was looking for something that didn't exist – at least not the way I had envisioned in my mind. I was trying to bake my Cake in an EZ Bake Oven™ with no real heat, fake ingredients, and a recipe designed for me by others.

How many times do we all get caught up in this type of existence? Things may look great on the outside, but we are a weepy mess on the inside and can't figure out why. We all have notions of what we 'should' be, based largely on the opinions of others. But, what do we really want? Sadly, most of us feel guilty asking what we want because we've been taught to believe it's selfish not to live for everyone else and take care of their needs. You can't be your best and help your friends and family to the best of your ability if you aren't truly happy yourself.

Throughout this book, you will find inspirational quotations, as well as some Bible quotes that have meant a lot to me. I have also included some suggested affirmations, which I call "Life Lessons." These are meant to inspire and encourage you. Sometimes, while going through some dark days, it was just a quote or inspirational story that kept me going, so I've added them here for you to hold on to as well. There are also plenty of places to jot down your own thoughts or ideas, as well as some workbook space at the end of the book to allow you to begin your unique journey and see your progress.

Baking up your sweet life cake is a process and in order to reap rewards, you will need to work through a lot of additives that have built up in your life. After all, our lives begin before we are born, and we spend years, sometimes decades getting to where we are now. We don't do that without making some mistakes and wrong turns along the way. We don't arrive where we are overnight and we can't fix it overnight. It's those mistakes (I now call them learning opportunities rather than mistakes) that make us stronger. We also have accomplished some great things in our lives and have joyful moments, and we need to remember those too. They are easy to forget when the dark days overshadow you.

So if your life is anything like mine, and you could use a little more sweetness, some inspiration, and a recipe for living life your way, this book is for you. It doesn't matter if that life is as a single cupcake, or a full out 7-layer extravaganza, with or without frosting you deserve to find joy, peace and happiness.

Now let's get baking!

Success is the sum of small efforts, repeated
day in and day out.
~ Robert Collier

Cake: Sherry Wilsher

*Optimist's Creed **

I Promise Myself...

To be so strong that nothing can disturb
my peace of mind.

*

To talk health, happiness, and prosperity
to every person I meet.

* *

To make all my friends feel that there is something
worthwhile in them.

*

To look at the sunny side of everything and make
my optimism come true.

* *

To think only of the best, to work only for the best
and to expect only the best.

*

To be just as enthusiastic about the success of others as I am
about my own.

* *

To forget the mistakes of the past and press on to
the greater achievements of the future.

*

To wear a cheerful expression at all times and give a
smile to every living creature I meet.

To give so much time to improving myself that I have no time to criticize others.

* *

To be too large for worry, too noble for anger, too strong for fear, and too happy to permit the presence of trouble.

*

To think well of myself and to proclaim this fact to the world, not in loud words, but in great deeds.

* *

To live in the faith that the whole world is on my side, so long as I am true to the best that is in me.

*

Original Text by Christian D. Larson 1912 (modified)

If you don't know where you are going, you'll end up someplace else.

~ Yogi Berra ~

1

Clearing out the Clutter

Prepping the Kitchen
to Make Way for Success

Yogi Berra was famous for his funny quotes, but there was often a kernel of profound truth at the center. One of my favorite Yogi Berra quotes is, "You gotta know where you're going in order to get there." In this quote, he was absolutely correct. We can just jump out into life having no clue as to the destination. The problem many of us have is that we have collected so much clutter in our lives that we don't have a clue what that new destination might be. So the first order of business is clearing the debris from your path.

I'm sure, like me, you've had trouble cooking in someone else's kitchen. Where are the spoons? How does this stove work? OH NO, there are no Italian herbs for the sauce! Very often, the kitchen itself is poorly organized, the counter space cluttered with small appliances, leftovers, and unopened mail. Who can cook in this environment?

Your mind is like that strange and cluttered kitchen. You will not be able to bake up a sweet life cake if your head is filled with leftovers. Old grudges, the remains of rotten relationships, past hurts, bad memories, negative self-images, and past failures are all the wrong ingredients for your new sweet life and they must be dealt with in order to move on.

Much of the clutter in our minds comes from what we learned as children, or from negative experiences. Like old recipes for liver and onions, they have to go. They have been discredited, have contributed to your unhappiness, and need to go the way of the dinosaur. We want new recipes. Fresh. Tasty. Substantial. Filled with flavor and spice. You won't have room to create something new if you don't first remove all the distractions that these old experiences and hurts bring to your life.

When you think of what you were told growing up, many of us weren't really in the generation that thought a woman's place was in the home. Worse, we were led to believe we could and should do it all – bring home the bacon, fry it up in the pan and then slide into the slinky negligee so he can get his groove on! Really? In what Universe was this superwoman supposed to exist? Yet because we believed this fantasy, many of us ended up tired, frustrated, and unhappy because we tried to live this ideal woman's life. Now's the time to toss this ridiculous wonder woman out on her butt. Get rid of the idea that you should be anything more than what you are. Release that self-imposed pressure to be everywhere, do everything and keep it all together. No one can do that, so now is the time to decide what is important to you, then make the choices to bring peace and joy back to your chaotic life.

It is okay to take time for you. It is okay to say no. It is okay to want to be happy. It may sound silly to read those sentences because most of us will say we already know those things. But we don't live it, which means that deep down we don't really believe it. Those old ideas that you should suffer in silence and get through it aren't helping you. In fact, they tear you apart bit by bit like waves cutting sand from under the cliff; eventually it falls into the sea. The same is true of you if you allow life to pile up on your shoulders and keep trudging along like some ancient martyr. You will buckle at some point, unless you learn to let go of all those burdens and allow your mind the freedom to take a simple break.

Find a quiet spot and release the worries that clutter your mind. It's a process and you can start right now by releasing what you are dealing with today. Close your eyes and breathe in. Now expel that breath and with it all the struggles of today. Don't worry about the big project at work next week, what time your son's soccer practice is, what to fix for dinner or even that your roots need a touch up. Let it all go and clear your mind. Give yourself the gift of a moment's peace.

Once your mind is free and clear, there will be lots of room for good memories to rise to the surface. For example, maybe you remember the thrill of accomplishment from the day you proudly graduated with a degree. Perhaps you remember that awesome trip to Cozumel when you walked along the beach and goose-bumps rippled across your skin at the wondrous beauty of a spectacular sunset. What about the joy of seeing your child's face for the first time the day he or she was born? Grasp onto those remembered feelings of joy, happiness, and excitement.

As you clear away all the worries, there will be space available for new concepts and ideas, and room to plan a great future. Most importantly, you will be able to discover what is really important to YOU, rather than what is important to others in your life. Only when you are happy, motivated, self-confident, and living your best life can you be successful, a good friend, supportive family member, or loving partner. The good life must be baked up from the inside; it cannot be imposed from the outside, like a layer of icing over a spoiled cake. There is an old saying in Texas: "Frosting a cow patty don't make it cake." This is so true, as we get trapped into making sure everything looks great on the outside, while we are barely keeping ourselves together on the inside.

The Couples' Society

Some of the clutter and old programming we each bring to the table includes the idea that this is a 'couple's society.' The expectation put upon both men and women is that we must have a partner to be whole and without one we are as unfinished and undesirable as unbaked cake batter. How many times have you heard or said something like this:

"She's pretty, but there must be something wrong with her. Look at her, sitting all by herself. Couldn't she get a date?"

No, and she didn't want one. In fact, she was asked out by several men, but she preferred to enjoy dinner and a glass of wine with only her thoughts for company.

She found that preferable to mindless small talk with someone who only wanted to sleep with her. It is okay to be by yourself in any situation, but we make ourselves and others feel awkward to be alone.

"Wow, she sounds smart, but
I don't know. Isn't she still single?"

Yes, she's single by choice. She chose to bake a single-layer cake to perfection rather than accepting a mediocre multi-layer cake with no taste or substance.

"Do you think she's gay? I don't think she's even had a date this year."

What a ridiculous question! The idea is that if she doesn't have a man, she must not want one and if she doesn't want a man then she must be gay. The correct conclusion should be that she only wants the right partner at the right time and has the self respect to wait for that person. She's being patient and selective rather than spending time and energy with someone who doesn't fit just to be a couple.

This kind of couples thinking has led both men and women to beg cousins to accompany them to the prom or special event, like a wedding, rather than stay home or go it alone. It has resulted in women purchasing 'companions' rather than be seen single at an event. It has also led to many generations of women and men who believe they are incomplete or viewed as less of a person if they do not have a partner on their arm. Nonsense!

It is vital to break the pattern of this programming. After all, isn't it better to stay home immersed in a fragrant bubble bath with a luscious cupcake than to go out with some half-baked beef cake?

I choose to view it this way:

Alone = All One

In other words, you are a solid entity, standing on your own. When you do choose a partner, it will be to make Two – a couple – not to complete yourself. You are complete. Never think otherwise, even though sometimes it can be hard. No matter how far our society has evolved, gender bias still prevails in almost every area of life. I'm not talking about equal work for equal pay or politics, though there are definitely still gender biases in those areas. What I am referring to is how we view single people and the fact that a single woman is still viewed in a negative light. Women are spinsters, old maids, or secret lesbians living a lonely or tawdry life, while men are bachelors, men about town and playboys. More nonsense! Men often hate this stereotype as much as women do. Why should they have to put up with some mindless Chatty Kathy just so the family won't think he's weird?

These societal pressures are important because when we think these things about people, it is inevitable when we are in that same situation, being single, we think those negative things about ourselves. We wonder what is wrong with us and often seek any date just to say we have someone interested, even if they are a totally bad fit for us. It's almost like you work yourself into a frenzy and it attracts the worst sort who can smell that desperation like fresh shark bait. At a time when we are the most vulnerable, we open ourselves up to situations and events that can cause lasting damage and trauma to our true selves for no other reason than what others might think and to keep ourselves from feeling lonely.

This type of pressure to find a mate caused me to go from living in my father's home and under his care and direction to living with my husband. I never took time to be alone and live alone. To find out who I really was, what I wanted out of life, and what gifts I had to offer the world. I never learned how to stand alone, as 'all one.'

Those around me considered marriage to be an achievement and confirmation that I was an adult, I was happy and excited to rush toward a marriage that was not right for me as a person. That is a very difficult thing to undo once you are in it and I'm not intimating that it was easy. It was very hard and there were a lot of tears, sleepless nights and terrible angst, especially when I realized my real solution was to move on after over two decades. While I knew it was right for me, it was difficult not to feel like a failure.

If you divorce in a 'couples' society, it is often seen as failure. It gives the impression you are damaged goods. These are the types of ideas you must let go of to clear your mind and make room for peace and happiness. You have made choices, as have I - some good, some that were more learning experiences and that's okay. You have the option to pick yourself up, get back on the bus and keep moving forward in a better and more positive manner.

Clearing the clutter is basically removing anything and everything that is keeping you from your dreams. Some of those things may be small, like spending too much time with a negative friend. Others may be huge, like choosing to leave a long term relationship. You have to address them all, as if you were clearing out the clutter in your kitchen. You would toss everything stale, beyond its expiration date, broken, useless, not on your diet, or just plain unhelpful. In baking up your sweet life, it means getting rid of guilt from past choices and losing the victim mentality. You must visualize only positive images of that multi-layer luscious, sexy, sweet cake life that you are preparing in order to make it happen.

I really want to talk a little about the 'woe is me' club, also known as Martyrs Anonymous, because there are a lot of people who are members including me on occasion. Even the most positive people in the world can occasionally feel trampled by events and circumstances, but just because you fall in the mud does not mean you should wallow in it. In today's society, everyone wants to shift blame. We want to believe that whatever happens or happened is not our fault.

The problem with assessing blame is that it stops you in your tracks because it transfers the power in your life to someone else. If it's someone else's fault, then someone else has to fix it, and that is not going to happen. You are in control of your life and how you react to every single event, so that means that someone only has power over you if you give it to them. Blame is like handing over your life and stepping out of the picture. You never move beyond that point.

Life isn't about fault, and spending any of your time dwelling on who did what to whom is just a waste of your energy. The blame game leads nowhere sweet. Even if you were victimized by someone, whether it was a boss, lover, family member, or stranger, just toss it out with the rest of the garbage. There's no room in our cupboard for sour grapes or what might have been. It is a choice. Every time you think of an old hurt or injustice, you hold onto it and relive the negative emotion attached to that time in your life. Realize this does nothing but hurt you and only you can choose at any point to release it. In doing so, you choose to release yourself from bondage. Hanging on is like picking at a festering wound, it never has the possibility to heal.

As you remove more and more of this emotional clutter, you will fill your mind with carefully thought out ingredients right for you. The ones your gut tells you will be good for you. They are those things that inspire you, make you feel good and put a smile on your face.

It might be something such as learning a new language, or entering a health and fitness competition. You might run a marathon, write a book, be your son's Cub Scout den leader, organize a charity, be a shoulder for a friend, or just be happy in your own skin. It doesn't have to be something earth shattering. Sometimes it's something as simple as just sitting on your patio on a beautiful Saturday morning with your favorite cup of tea, listening to the birds sing. You have the ability to do, have, and be anything you choose. Every moment of your life is a choice, even when it doesn't feel like it. You can choose to be positive or negative and no one makes that choice but you.

We all live jam-packed lives and often it seems like there isn't possibly room for one more thing. This makes it necessary that you take the clutter you just got rid of and throw it away for good. Don't stuff it in a closet or spare room so you can come back and wallow later. Just like it feels great to get rid of your 'fat' clothes when you lose a few pounds, this will too. Don't keep the baggage out of some sense of security or because it's what you've always known. Once you make room in your life for good things, then they will flood in. But if you never make that room in your life, then you are squeezing out all the good stuff the Universe is just waiting to deliver.

Think of it this way: Pretend you are a pastry chef. A two-layer cake is created by placing one stand-alone layer atop another stand-alone layer. Each layer must be tasty and complete on its own. Putting them together merely makes the cake larger and more impressive, but each layer could be enjoyed individually. They do not merge, meld, or melt into each other but they are loosely attached with a thin layer of frosting.

This process of standing alone sometimes must be repeated throughout our lives, not only before that first marriage or serious commitment. Often following a divorce or breakup, it is necessary to find some solitude to reassess and relearn those critical lessons of single layer cake baking. Do not be afraid of that solitude. Embrace it, enjoy it, and use that space to grow and learn more about yourself as an individual. Denying yourself this wonderful pleasure is the ultimate act of emotional mutilation. We need some time to develop, like yeast in warm water, and figure out our strengths and what type of cake we want to be. Remember it's the cake, you, that yearns to be tasty, substantial, and fully baked. We can choose to frost or not, based on our own needs and wants but we can't skip the baking

The Junk Yard

As a child, I was exposed to many 'not to dos.' My parents were young and made mistakes, as parents will do on occasion. I know they tried hard to be good parents but struggled in many ways – it's not like there were any kind of parenting classes back then. It took several years after becoming an adult for me to finally figure out that they'd done the best they could under the circumstances.

The hindsight that maturity offers can be a wonderful thing. I also found out in my later years that the childhoods of both my parents were very traumatic. This explained a lot about their individual strengths and weaknesses. Before I discovered this truth, I was the grand master of the blame game, blaming them for many of my problems.

The best part about my discoveries about myself, is that I now got to choose how I viewed my parents and how I was raised. So, instead of holding onto that blame, I chose to change my view of them. I chose to appreciate their efforts and understand how hard they tried in the wake of their own difficult experiences. I forgave them for things I saw as their shortcomings and a great weight was lifted from my shoulders allowing me to love them unconditionally for the first time.

It took years to evolve to where I am today. I have reprogrammed many of my beliefs that didn't serve me or that were false. Like layers of a beautiful cake, each life experience has provided me with the different ingredients to have the most tasteful cake. Though it came through much trial and error, I am finally discovering the right amount of flavor needed from each ingredient to make my cake exactly what I want it to be but it is, and will always be, an ongoing process.

My life is assaulted by daily tribulations just like everyone else's – traffic woes, difficult clients, relationship ups and downs as well as many other little bumps in the road. Every once in a while I find myself in certain situations and stuck in patterns that I recognize as not beneficial to me. When that occurs, I search for the root of the issue, and sometimes it's as simple as recognizing that I still strive for some idea of perfection that is unattainable.

I know deep down the best I can do is good enough yet it still rears its ugly little head like a big lump in my cake batter. Recognition of those recurring issues and patterns of behavior is the first step and you will always need to be vigilant to cut those negative beliefs and habits off at the knee.

Core happiness is the underlying fuel that drives my mission to make my life better. To wake knowing life is good right now is something I have to remind myself to do, as my ego tends to want to always be productive which leads me to the many distractions and 'busyness' I sometimes fall in to.

I'll be the first to admit that it can be hard to recognize your own past programming because it is so ingrained. However, there are some tip offs that you can recognize to determine if some of your behaviors might be rooted in beliefs that don't move your life to a more positive place.

Addictive Behaviors

Do you ever feel like you have to be in the company of others (or one particular person) or you're going to die? Or, that you need to fill your life with rituals and a busy schedule to feel complete? Perhaps you're a shopaholic and believe that the next new outfit will cure all your ills?

Addictive behaviors don't just have to do with substance abuse – although they certainly can. When we feel a loss or that something is missing in our lives, human nature is that we want to feel better so we turn to things or behaviors that at least temporarily help produce that feeling. This is often destructive and causes more problems than it cures. It's true that some people may turn to drugs or alcohol, but more often we fall back on behaviors such as shopping, starting new relationships or creating such 'busyness' in our lives that we can't really think about our problems. On the surface these behaviors may not seem like such a big deal, but when we are hurting we tend to take them to extremes, creating additional problems such as financial issues, strained relationships and exhaustion or burnout.

In short, your life is completely unbalanced and deep down you know when this happens. You have trouble sleeping and want to run away. That is one of the signs to pay attention to and realize that there is no substitute for happiness. It comes from within. You can never fix it by buying more stuff, finding a new person or being more perfect.

I went through an especially rough time in my own life when my marriage failed and I suffered big financial losses. I had to start over from scratch as if the previous twenty years hadn't happened. I struggled with pure loneliness for several months, faking smiles wherever I went. I was dying on the inside.

My heart was weighed down with a pain so intense it was sure to show up in my daily experiences. I know what it's like to fear that kind of pain. I can also tell you that part of the growth experience toward a new life is not only experiencing those feelings, but learning how to overcome them. Avoiding the emotions doesn't work and they will resurface if not dealt with in a positive fashion.

The secret to overcome my negative experiences and emotions had one hundred percent to do with attitude. Really, that's all I had. I was starting over with nothing, so every morning I reminded myself that today, right now, was a wonderful time in my life and I would triumph over the past by letting it go and choosing to be happy. You have to believe that it is possible to heal and achieve total happiness. Then each day it becomes more and more real to you. Over time you find that you have cleared all those old emotions and now are not only moving forward, but that you are doing so in a way that is whole and complete.

Am I Ready or Just Lonely?

This question is one that surfaced since my 'All One' journey began. Some of my negative experiences had to do with relationships and when coupled with those ideas I'd previously had of not being whole without a partner, I knew I wanted this time to be different. I wanted to break that cycle of old ideas and dependency on another person to complete me. But how does someone know when they are ready to put themselves back out there and look for that healthy relationship? There is a definite way to find out the answer to this by asking yourself, "If I put myself out there and find a match, and it goes well at first but soon fizzles, will this devastate me or do I see it as opportunity to grow until the right relationship surfaces?"

How you react to a breakup will be the indicator of where you are on the readiness scale. If you know without a doubt you'll be fine regardless of the outcome, then that will determine your status of Ready or Just Lonely. Lonely represents the need to be fulfilled by another. This feeling can be relieved by the company of someone else; however, you must realize your happiness is not up to another. No one can 'make' you happy and you can't 'make' anyone else happy. That is a choice we all make for ourselves.

If you expect someone to make you happy, they will fail every time. Only when you are ready to be happy alone can you be happy with someone else.

> *When you forgive, you heal your own anger and hurt and are able to let love lead again. It's like spring cleaning for your heart.*
> *~ Marci Shimoff*

Cake: Sherry Wilsher

Exercise #1:

To help you clear the old ideas, programming and experiences (clutter) from your mind, find a quiet place, close your eyes, and take three deep breaths in and out. Now say the following affirmation several times.

An Affirmation for Clearing out the Clutter:

Piece by piece, I let go of those things that no longer serve a positive purpose in my life to allow room for the rich blessings which are rightfully mine.

*NOTES:

The following space is for listing those things that may be cluttering your life and blocking your journey. Note each issue you feel is blocking your progress, then also note how you plan to clear them away!

_____

_____

_____

_____

_____

_____

_____

_____

_____

_____

*If I am not for myself, who will be?
And if I am for myself alone, then
what am I? And if not now, when?*

- Rabbi Hillel, Pirke Avot 1:14

2

Designing a Recipe for Success

No Half-Baked Dreams in Our Kitchen!

* *

*W*hen I was young, I thought about what happiness looked like and how I would accomplish my own happiness. Marriage seemed like the right answer, the only answer really, since I was taught from a small girl that I could only be happy if I "found a good man." Were you brain washed, conditioned, and cream rinsed too? Marriage was just what women did not so many decades ago; they were primarily the homemakers and depended upon a man for their security, livelihood, identity, companionship, sex, and general well-being. They were the unsung heroines a la Harriet Nelson and other iconic TV housewives, setting the pearl and apron wearing standard for all proper young women to follow.

Then awareness that women can be much more than that rose, thanks to pioneers and bold women who believed they need not limit themselves to homemaking and childcare, unless they chose to. Today we take for granted that women have unlimited options, yet I think there is still lingering doubt in many a female psyche because we still hold in our minds this idea of the perfect life.

You know who you are. You're the one who would rather stay home on New Year's Eve than go to a party dateless. You're the one who feels ever so much better if there's a male pilot in the cockpit or a male doctor holding the scalpel.

These dramatic societal changes take a long time, many generations, to manifest themselves fully and they take just as long to change. While you may not voice your thoughts, they do have an emotional effect on you.

I followed the societal norms and the nudging of my family, and at the very young age of 22 I found a decent guy and got married. It seemed the thing to do, the next step. I remember looking at myself in the mirror on my wedding day, and telling myself, "If this doesn't work out, there's always divorce."

What kind of woman thinks of divorce on her wedding day? Which by the way, was not a real wedding at all. Due to pressures, I asked myself, 'What will others think if we are living together without being married?' So, we decided to please them all and tie this frayed knot at the local courthouse, in front of the Justice of the Peace.

Right from the beginning, something was missing. As often happens when we are nose to nose with a problem, we lose perspective. I had no clue what the problem was. I searched, but it was like trying to grasp smoke in a windstorm. Eventually I became detached from my own pursuit of happiness and started living my life solely for others. I was so afraid of facing the loneliness and uncertainty that might engulf me if I left. I endured my empty life for many years and tried to accept it. I told myself 'that's the way things are' and I needed to get a grip and get on with life.

I have met many women who typify this martyr syndrome, but most of it comes down to one issue - they are terrified to be alone.

Much more terrified of that aspect than staying in a bad situation. Even though their marriages are miserable, they still walk on eggshells for fear of upsetting their lifeline (meal ticket). I have sympathy for them, but want to shake them out of their inertia. I want to shout, "Wake up!"

Like me, until they recognize their lives are what they have chosen, and that they do have a choice, no one else can change their path. I have to remain on my own journey and hopefully they too will come to the awareness that life can be so much sweeter. Being alone can offer great relief from the stressful unhappy life they may be experiencing. There is something affirming and validating to have complete say over your time, your actions, your money and every other aspect of life. Sure, it is scary to be out there on your own, but somehow it's so much better than trying to hold a bad situation together.

A marriage should be a partnership, not indentured servitude, or a draining habit. Either be better together, or be better apart, but make the choice with deliberation and self-confidence. Yes, it is very intimidating to take that leap of faith, but it can be the most wonderful flight of freedom. It is empowering, enlivening, spiritual, and rewarding all at the same time.

No one can be truly happy staying in a negative emotionally sickening situation. If you feel emotionally beat up, trapped, or fearful, it is time to change things up and find peace. To stay in the marriage and fix it requires both partners to want change and you can't force anyone else to change. You also can't keep making excuses for them or justifying behaviors that are damaging to your well being.

Now, don't think I'm only talking about women here! Men also get stuck in this trap of unhappiness. Many of them were brought up with the idea that their responsibility is to provide. They were never told they deserve to be happy too. They live in a hollow shadow of a relationship while their own needs languish, which leads to anger and bitterness. I know you've seen those couples who exude bitterness and condescension. No one wants to be around them because they are so unhappy and it is obvious to everyone but them that they should be apart. Hopefully, this book will help some of you face the reality of your current situation and give you the courage to make choices that are in your best interest for the long term. I did it, so can you!

We all hide from the truth, and I was no different. In fact I was the queen of denial in every respect for a lot of years. You may recognize some of the things I did to detach myself from facing the truth:

1. I told myself every problem
with my marriage was my fault.

This is easy to believe, especially if you are with someone who frequently points out your weaknesses. Make no mistake I do, and did, have faults, but I also see that it takes two people to create a problem and two people to fix it, and if just one is trying then it's a hopeless endeavor. Marriage should enhance and uplift each person and if someone, or both parties, are constantly in 'tear down' mode then it's very destructive.

Many times this destruction is hidden in humor and so we think if it's funny, that it's okay, but it's not. Over time it stops being funny and is damaging. Is a laugh worth destroying your marriage or the self esteem of the person you are supposed to love?

2. I blamed my parents.

Again this is easy to do because it keeps you from taking responsibility for your part in things and it keeps you from having a confrontation with your partner. I hated confrontation. We might like to believe that we can't help our behaviors and because our parents raised us, then it's all their fault. The truth is that once we are adults we choose what we believe and how we behave. No matter what your past experiences, they are no excuse not to take responsibility for your present reality.

Playing this sort of blame game also cheats you out of a positive relationship with your parents, as well as your children, and that just causes everyone more hurt. Its also common for people to blame other experiences, like being hurt in a previous relationship. So they use that as an excuse to withhold or not be fully invested in a current relationship, but this, too, is destructive. We all have bad experiences. We choose if we will allow them to taint our future happiness or not.

3. I looked to fill the void
of love in another way.

In my case, I decided to have a baby, believing that this new little person would love me unconditionally and fill the void left by an empty life. I dearly love my child. But I will tell you that my needing someone to love me was not a good reason to bring another person into the world. I was very lucky as I share a love with my son that is unmatched and unconditional. However, during the course of his life, I was not the happiest person on the planet because then I had even more responsibility and commitments. It made my feelings of unhappiness deepen rather than solve them. I was overwhelmed, though I was doing the best I could under the circumstances. All in all, it turned out well. Jacob is a very responsible young man; I am extremely proud to be his mother and his friend. I know he had to experience some of these life lessons along with me and those were not the best experiences for a young person. I am grateful for his patience and strength through it all. What a blessing he is and has always been in my life!

Another person that is outside the marriage cannot fill the void the marriage should. This includes a child, but it also includes friends and other relationships. It's not uncommon for a spouse to seek that emotional bond elsewhere, either through a deep friendship with someone else, or even through an affair.

None of these will ever fill the void or make that need for love from your spouse go away and they always cause more problems than they solve. Yet many people regularly engage in a series of outside relationships rather than get out of an unhappy marriage. It may be guilt, or some misguided sense of obligation that keeps them holding on to something that is clearly gone. In the long run it creates much more hurt than getting a divorce and moving on would have.

4. I became a workaholic.

I dove head first into my work, working long hours to numb my feelings and avoid facing the truth. This is one area both men and women gravitate toward when other areas in their life aren't going well. It is easy to keep yourself so busy every day that you don't have time to think about your problems, feel bad, or dwell on the fact you aren't happy. Work is an escape, but because we are being productive and earning more money, we often think that it's okay. But it's not. Problems that are denied or ignored only get bigger, they don't go away.

Working too much is typical avoidance behavior and we all do it to some extent. When we are in a difficult relationship, it is so easy to escape and so hard to recognize how damaging it can be. That's because work produces some positive results in our lives and as I worked harder my income went up – which felt like a great thing! In truth, it was just bad ingredients as I was covering over the real problem and trying to make it all look great with my higher income and more stuff. The problem still lay under the surface simmering and building.

5. I stuffed my feelings with food.

Food became solace as I sought to fill the empty spaces within my soul with gooey calories and rich foods. Again, this is behavior that both men and women frequently engage in when emotional issues arise. Men are taught not to cry or show emotions, but they are also encouraged to eat and be a 'big, healthy guy', and because of this you see a lot of overweight men who are really hurting inside.

Women commonly feed emotion with food, and I did too. There is nothing like squishing yourself into your favorite pair of jeans only to realize you now look like a stuffed sausage. And it happens so quickly. Food soothes, but then makes us feel even worse later because not only are we unhappy about our lives, we are now self conscious about how we look. It is also an obvious outward sign that something isn't right and as such brings a certain amount of embarrassment and shame as people around you start to inquire if you are okay. Like anything else, excessive food is a bad ingredient and can't replace happiness.

6. I became an exercise freak.

My overeating, and the scrutiny it brought, led to fanatical exercise sessions to lose the extra pounds. One of my biggest issues was this idea in my mind that I had to be 'perfect.' As soon as I slapped on those pounds from the luscious desserts that had·become my new emotional support, I went into an exercising frenzy to get rid of the extra pounds. I can see how so many women end up with eating disorders, but here again they are the manifestation of the unhappiness they are experiencing in their lives, just as it was in my life.

This is also an activity that seems 'good' on the outside, but taken to extremes can be destructive to the relationship as exercise is an escape just like work can be. Men can really get caught in this exercise trap very easily as they are also told by society that being fit is good. So you will often see them get into bodybuilding or marathon running or other such sports. The next thing you know, they are in the gym or out running every waking hour and are now absent spouses. We all justify this activity because its 'good' and can't understand why our spouses get annoyed. We are improving ourselves, right? But there is a balance to be struck. When you are out of balance, then it's just an escape from the relationship and that is what your spouse is noticing.

7. I became a little obsessive compulsive.

As my life got more difficult, I obsessed over my appearance and became a shopaholic, spending too much money on too many things I didn't need. This was truly detrimental in many ways. Shopping gives you a euphoric feeling much like eating your favorite donuts or exercising. I got that same high when I bought something great. But then many of those items would hang in my closet with the tags on for months or even years. It wasn't about me needing more stuff. It wasn't about the money. It was about the comfort I got from it and that had to be addressed.

There are many areas and ways in your life that some kind of obsessive compulsive behavior can manifest itself. Maybe you are a gambler and you start to gamble more than you can afford to lose. Maybe you are an animal lover and start taking in more animals than is healthy. Maybe you clean your home within an inch of its life everyday and lie awake at night wondering if it's clean.

These may sound like extreme behaviors, but they can easily appear when you are feeling low and unloved. I've known men in an unhappy marriage gamble their life savings on risky business deals, or engage in thrill seeking of the life-threatening variety, such as sky diving or intense mountain climbing. It doesn't really matter what the behavior is, if it starts to become extreme or causes additional stress in your relationship then you must take a step back and look at things as objectively as possible. Is it improving your life? Is it moving you forward? Does it enhance your relationship? In my case, the answer to all of those questions was no because I was just trying to make myself happy and didn't really care about the consequences.

8. I became a martyr.

I tried to do for others constantly, anxiously wanting to please them and gain acceptance. I wanted to make everyone happy. I like to call this my "Mary the Martyr" tendency. It is satisfying to do for others and I like that feeling. When I was in this mindset, however, a lot of doing for others was done out of pure guilt. Were you brought up to believe it is better to give than to receive? Remember, you gotta have to be able to give. This goes for love, money, encouragement, or any number of things we feel we must do to please everyone. If you are the kind of person who enjoys doing good deeds for others, make sure you are doing them for the right reasons. Often, in a bad or languishing relationship, it's easy to feel unwanted, unneeded and unloved. When you help others they praise you and it is like feeding an addiction. Your heart is so parched that any drop of kindness or notice from others is like a drug. Doing for others is a good thing, which is why it can be hard to recognize as one of the signs that you have emotional needs that are withering away.

9. I found a pill for it.

In our world today, if you want something there is an app for it or a pill to fix it. For me, prescription mood stabilizers were the next rung of the downward ladder, after food and shopping failed. Eventually, no matter how many tactics I tried to make myself feel better, I ended up unhappier than ever, not to mention run down and stressed out. Constantly drained, both physically and emotionally, I knew if it continued I would cease to function. My next stop was to the doctor to see what was wrong.

He prescribed some pills that would perk me up and help me be happier. They made me seem a little happier, but they didn't make the situation better. I'm not saying that these medications are bad or not necessary in some situations, they did help me for a time. But in my case they also allowed me to continue to avoid the real problem, so they were like a bandage on a raw open wound that needed stitches. It's easy to see how someone can spiral downward to addiction as they seek stronger and stronger drugs to cover the wounds and soothe their lonely, broken heart.

10. I was never alone.

Above all, I avoided solitude at all costs, doing anything and everything to avoid being alone with the real me. Not only was I not ready to bake myself a sweet life, I would not even preheat the oven! I stayed in a chilly relationship, one that lacked warmth and passion, because I was so afraid of solitude. I was very social and sought out ways to be with others in yet another attempt to avoid my relationship and get the social interaction and friendship that I wasn't getting at home. It didn't matter what the event was, if there were others around then I could focus on chatting and having a good time with them and leave my unhappiness and emptiness behind – but only for a while.

These behaviors were some that I encountered and yours may be similar or you may have other behaviors that aren't listed here. As long as you identify them as something damaging or that is not moving you forward then you can help yourself toward a better life. But it is a process and not easy. Don't think that you will just wake up one day and change your life in every aspect. For most people it doesn't work like that, it is a process.

One day, after several failed attempts to leave the relationship, I had a burst of confidence and I finally made a clean break from my marriage. It was the scariest thing I ever did; it was like walking off a cliff with only sky above and empty air below. If you've ever had that 'falling' dream, you know what I mean. It was so terrifying that I nearly ran back to him, but some kernel of courage, a tiny inner flame, motivated me to strike out on my own and stick to the road I had chosen.

This little detail may not seem worth sharing, but I know it is because so many people experience insecurity and uncertainty. Women and men both can relate to the boomerang effect of getting one foot out the door, then beating a hasty retreat back to the old and familiar nest. 'Better the devil you know' takes hold than fear of the unknown overwhelms us. Loneliness and the prospect of making choices during this time can cause havoc in your life and make your cake fall flat.

I remember telling my closest friends, "Anyone attracted to me right now has to have problems of their own." This is true for anyone going through a major life change because there is damage left by the trauma that needs to heal. Damaged people attract damaged people because they see that same desperation and insecurity. So, I kept clear of allowing anyone in my life longer than the time it takes for brief introductions or the most superficial interactions. I felt so incomplete at times and knew anyone that showed interest in me, was probably experiencing life exactly the same way, if not worse.

This is why so many people get out of one bad situation and then hop right back into another very similar one. They haven't taken the time to evaluate their behaviors and decide what they really want. Then they have a hard time showing the discipline to wait for that better relationship to come along. Some women talk about how they got out of a bad marriage and the next thing you know they are married again to exactly the same type of man they divorced. Even though they didn't go back to their first husband, they sought out the familiar and even though it was negative, it was comfortable.

I thought getting involved with someone as screwed up as I was would be a disaster. My theory proved to be correct. I quickly discovered that the few men I let get to know me, even a little, were experiencing setbacks resulting from failed relationships, fear of relationships, or lacked self-confidence. Two messes combined do not make a clean kitchen or a sweet experience!

I remember thinking, filled with doubt as usual, but he's so cute! Then, well, I could be called cute too. Just because the cake looks delicious on the outside, just like the displays in the bakery window, there could be nothing but a cardboard box underneath all of that beautiful frosting. That goes for men and women both in social and business settings. You have to look beneath the frosting for what's real. It is hard to say no when someone wants to compliment and dote on you, but you have to recognize that it is just a temporary bandage and will cause you much more harm than good in the long run.

I truly believe that once a person finds him/herself in their own state of bliss without doing it for anyone else but themselves, they will attract their heart's desires and that perfect relationship will be drawn to them. It is something I look forward to experiencing and welcome it when my cake is fully baked and delicious, which means when the time is right.

Follow Your Own Recipe

Personal success and designing a good recipe for achieving it, depends on a combination of 'dry' rational actions and 'wet' emotional actions (tears.) We've all known people who were as dry as rice cakes or as wet as pudding and neither extreme leads to happiness. The best cake recipes require both types of ingredients and aim for a great blend or balance. Make sure you know which you have now, which you need to work on or obtain, and how to focus on one set vs. the other as necessary. For example, you may get 'dry' and logical at the first sign of a conflict, to reduce the importance of emotional baggage and protect yourself from feelings that might be negative. If this describes you, then you will need to think back on the experiences of your life and pinpoint a defeating experience that lead to this behavior. Maybe you were told repeatedly by your father that girls are too emotional and thus you tried very hard to be logical. Or, if you are overly emotional perhaps you were labeled a 'drama queen' by your family and thus they gave into you more easily. This worked for you as a child, but now it causes chaos in your relationships.

Once you identify the causes behind your behaviors, then it is important to outline steps to take to move forward in a healthy way. This is critical to long term balance and success. You can't allow yourself to chicken out and say 'well, that's the way I am.' You choose how you are today and you choose how you will be tomorrow. You can change, but only if you choose to. You must understand that if you don't change, or the results in your life don't change, that it is because you made the choice to accept that way of life and not improve. There's no escaping or blaming anyone else. The future is completely up to you and your happiness is at stake.

As women, we tend to be emotional creatures, often thinking with our hearts instead of our heads. This is not a bad thing, but to be successful in business and relationships, it is best to keep these ingredients (logic and emotions) separate until the appropriate time. What many of us do is allow one or the other to run our lives and once you mix them together in the wrong combination, there's no going back .You can't re-separate them. The damage is done. You may have to start all over again if you let your emotions reign supreme and eclipse rational decision making and the same is true if you make such cut and dried logical decisions that you don't listen to your own heart. The balance of both is key.

Fearful Fran or Betty Brave?

When deciding to change the direction of my life, I soon realized there were two sides to my story. There was the side that was represented by fear, and the other side that was represented by spirit. I often felt like a racehorse trapped in the gate; filled with energy and desire for a different life, but fearing what lay beyond. Would I win the race, or stumble, fall, make a fool of myself?

From a very young age I wished for a different life than what I had been born into. I made a conscious decision to do things differently than what I saw in my daily life. I didn't have a clue, of course, what that something different was, I just knew what I was experiencing was not it. I was in a bed of thorns and wanted relief from the prickles, but had no plan for climbing up and out. I had made the decision but I didn't have the action side of the equation down yet.

Decision + Action = Moving Forward

Question: Three birds are sitting on a wire. One bird decides to leave. How many are left?

Answer: Three. Just because one bird decides to leave, doesn't mean it'll actually do it!

The unsure little girl that still resides inside of me sometimes tries to run my show on occasion and I call her Fearful Fran. She constantly whispers in my ear all the what ifs and possible negative outcomes. Often she wins. However, when I notice Fran is getting me in trouble and keeping me from experiencing all I want from life, I mentally place a piece of tape over her mouth and place her in the corner. This is because while there is that spirit and drive, fear will paralyze and frustrate me. That fear comes from that little girl inside saying, "What if the worst happens?" or

"What will people think?" or "Haven't you tried that before and been a big fat failure?" We all have those inner voices. Sometimes they show our true desires and must be listened to, and sometimes they feed our fear and inertia and must be ignored. Part of baking your best sweet life cake is learning the difference.

When I took the actual steps necessary to move out and become independent, I was referred to as selfish be'och. This came from various corners – friends, family and of course the ever-present rumor mill. How could I be such a selfish person? What kind of woman decides she wants to run away from such a supposed great guy, in search of her own so-called happiness? As I moved forward with determination, the urge to be influence by or feel sorry for others faded. I was able to resist the cries from those in my previous life trying to distract me from my mission of independence. I had always catered to them in order to keep the peace and avoid the painful feeling of being alone. I realized that was hurting me and it was also hurting them by allowing things to remain dysfunctional.

Their name calling and bad attitude toward my happiness was nothing more than selfishness on their part, not mine. They benefited when I waited on them hand and foot and stood aside to let them be the stars. It was merely an attempt to bully me back into my 'place' as they defined it. But no one can define your place. You do that and by giving yourself room to grow, those around you will eventually grow too, whether they want to or not.

With the decision to create a stronger Sherry with confidence and vision, I adopted the philosophy of 'There's a new sheriff in town' and she is calling the shots now! As I worked hard to become stronger, an emotional tug-of-war raged inside of me between Fearful Fran and my Betty Brave persona that was moving ahead with confidence. Sweet little Sherry of old was still very much present and very concerned by the new version of me that was so desperate to find her way to the surface. For the first time in my life, I understood Multiple Personality Disorder; there was definitely a battle for control between the person I was in my old life and the person I truly could become. Of course this is a dramatization but the emotions felt that strong and that real at times! Change is not easy and there are always parts of us that yearn for the status quo. It's always so much easier to sit back in a safe place rather than make a decision with a goal in mind and go for it with full force. In other words, we can allow our lives to be ruled by chance (go with the flow) instead of taking the bull by the horns and forging our own path.

Ideas long suppressed bubbled to the surface, swarming like bees around a honeycomb in my mind. Each idea that had once plagued my mind was being addressed individually. I finally understood why I was never satisfied and cleaned even the dark dusty corners of my mind to root out anything that might interfere with the person I wanted to be. I discovered that as a garden has to be tended to daily in order to keep the weeds from taking over, I had to remove the emotional weeds in my life on a daily basis so my new-found inspirations could grow.

I also discovered (and this did not happen overnight – neither Rome nor Sherry was built in a day), the 'Cinderella ending' I always desired, or thought I did, was pure fiction. It was not only unrealistic; it was not even what I really wanted. The more I searched for it, the more miserable I became. If I couldn't find my Prince Charming, I thought, I could not be happy. How wrong I was! Prince or no Prince, I wanted to have my cake and eat it too. No one really wants to be the answer to someone else's fantasy ideal of how things should be anyway, because no real person could ever measure up. Not only was this fairy tale detrimental for me, it was also detrimental to those I wanted to have a relationship with. No real man wants to be compared to some prince on a horse and no real woman wants to try and be a 'princess' at five in the morning with no make-up and morning breath!

My Life's Recipe has Changed

Repeating affirmations and changing underlying beliefs will change your life. This I know to be true, because I lived it. I was a hot mess when I left my husband, but I changed and became the kind of happy fulfilled person that I'd always hoped to be. Now I'm living my own version of the sweet life and from this side looking back, I had no idea how hard it would be nor how glad I would be that I undertook the journey. It won't come overnight and it isn't always easy, but it is worth every ounce of effort you put into it. I think when you make great strides in your life and find that internal happiness, you look back and realize how big that is, but you also know that it is very do-able.

One of the greatest influences on my new life recipe was a film and set of DVDs titled *What the Bleep Do We Know*, *Down the Rabbit Hole*, respectively. Not one opinion or voice, these programs will introduce you to fourteen or more scientists, thinkers, and many revelations that will surprise and cause you to think. Some of you will relate to this, and others, you may question it. Either is fine, what is important is that the process leads to self evaluation, which is always valuable. You will gain insight and inspiration from dramatic film, documentary, animation, and comedy that serves up a mind-blowing menu of Quantum Physics, spirituality, neurology and evolutionary thought. If that sounds heavy, don't worry, it's really all about why we feel the way we do and how much control we really have over the results in our life and that is wonderfully inspiring information. You can take small bites, but I guarantee once you get a taste, you'll want more.

You will discover, as I did, some great insights into the human mind and how it plays out in the time/space reality. How the Universe is the result of the Universal Mind (GOD); how our thoughts, or our actual sub-consciously programmed beliefs, bring on what we experience.

For example:

You know (or are) that person that seems to attract chaos and drama. They go to a party and get things spilled on them. Birds choose their new car to take a dump on. They miss their flight on vacation. Why do these things seem to come in waves? The principles you will hear in the movies and teachings I recommended in the last paragraph will help you understand that we bring many of these things on ourselves. This was a revelation to me. Sometimes it seemed like life was making Sherry its personal dumping ground! In evaluating various situations I realized that I attracted much of what I thought was random happenstance because I was in 'Mary the Martyr' mode. This 'poor me' mindset resulted in my experiencing more crap every day.

This is a complex and difficult concept to grasp, yet I find it extremely interesting. Since learning this sort of 'you bring it on yourself' concept, any time something unpleasant happens to me, instead of feeling sorry for myself, I question why it happened in general, and why it happened to me specifically. I search for the root cause instead of only looking at the end result. It takes work, but I usually can find my answer quickly and once I take responsibility for it, then things change for the better.

This might be something to think about in your journal. Keep notes about anything negative that happens to you – date, time, what led up to it – and see if you can spot patterns of your own behavior and thought processes that might be causing or attracting these events.

Two Sides to Your Story: Spiritual and Human

Which side is leading you? Which side is in charge? Heart or Mind? Our soul, our spirit – that untouchable, enigmatic, mysterious part of our being – is the life force that propels us. Many believe that it is also the only part of us that transcends physical life. We also have our physical bodies, part of which is our mind. Are you driven and controlled by your human mind, or by your inner spirit?

The mind, because it is human, is flawed; filled with ego and therefore tends to want to run the show. However, when my human side leads the way I typically end up in a mess and calling on Spirit/God to get me out of it. Have you ever asked yourself, "How in the world did this happen?" or "How did I end up here?" I know I have, many times. I have also experienced my life with my spirit running the show, and when I allow this, life is always smooth.

You may be saying:

"Well, if I let spirit lead, what's the big deal?"

Try it and see. If you are not used to practicing deliberate living, spend one whole day letting spirit lead – it is an eye opening and self-affirming experience.

We intuitively know certain things when we meet someone or are put in a certain situation. I have experienced this often, as I'm sure you have too. This is our spirit/intuition trying to tell us something. When you meet someone you get an immediate impression of who they are, if they are honest, and if there are any hidden issues. There are frequently those little red flags or warning bells we experience, but our human side often forces those aside. As parents, especially as mothers, we have a connection to our children that is unmatched. We know when they are in trouble, when they are too quiet, or when something is wrong. It is something way beyond intuition or personal connection. Our spirits are linked tightly together.

The interesting thing is that we can have much of that same insight into others if we allow it. But we are distrustful of our own initial impressions many times and allow our human side to convince us that those 'feelings' aren't real or aren't important. That connection is far beyond what most of us experience on a daily basis, but with practice it can become an invaluable part of our lives and our experience.

This becomes even more important as we seek to be more in tune with who we are and what we want. By allowing our spiritual side to connect with others and living on purpose each day, we can easily evaluate people's motivations and intentions saving us literally years of a bad relationship or years of searching for the right person only to pass them over.

There are two things to aim at in life; first to get what you want, and after that to enjoy it. Only the wisest of mankind has achieved the second.
~ Logan Pearsall Smith

An Affirmation for Designing a
Recipe for Success:

Today I choose life.
Today, I am happy with my choices and
know they are the best for me.

Exercise #2:

Think about your emotional and logical side. Who is in charge most of the time? Write down those situations then think back to why you habitually allow one or the other to be in control. Think back to an event that might have been the instigator.

Now think about your human and spiritual side. Spend a day consciously allowing your spirit to lead. Set aside judgments and external influences and let your intuition give you insight into the people around you and the events you encounter. Write down your experience.

*NOTES:

*Destiny is no matter of chance.
It is a matter of choice: It is not a
thing to be waited for, it is a thing to
be achieved.
~ William Jennings Bryan*

Choose Your Style

& Yes, Size Matters

*D*o you want an individual cupcake, small but exquisite and unique? Or would you rather create a complex layer cake with many flavors? Perhaps your ideal sweet life would consist of a cozy single layer, pure vanilla, but uncomplicated and quite rich? What about a fancy Bundt cake with interesting shapes and dense consistency?

These are all very legitimate desires but most importantly, you want to choose your desire and one that should not ever be subjugated to the desires of others. It's okay to have lots of people in your life; people you love, care deeply about, and want happiness for as well. But their desires should not wash away yours, because if they do, they will end up with a "you" that they never anticipated and that you are not happy with.

Many women, most of them actually, believe that one plus one does not equal two. They believe that one plus one equals one. That when we become wives, partners, and soul mates, we join together and meld into one entity. 'Couple' becomes a codeword for 'us'. There is no longer a 'you', just an 'us'. Men, for some reason, tend to retain their individual identity for the most part, especially outside the home. That is to their credit. We often sit at home like some truncated limb, awaiting their return to make us whole again or worse, get mad at them for their individuality and demand they stop. Everything we want as individuals is often put on 'pause'. Once there are children, this is especially true for women as our focus becomes their lives, once again subjugating our own desires and needs for those of others.

Many of us initially choose this because we want to. We want to be there every second of every day of our children's lives, but by making that the only focus we are cheating ourselves out of happiness and cheating our children from the example of a happy, well balanced mother. Not to mention the fact that the relationship that produced that child gets tossed aside like yesterday's stale bread heaping stress on everyone.

I hear the same things from other women so I know it's not just me. Typically at the salon during a pedicure for instance, women open up and talk about their lives and how they are lost and don't know what they are going to do when the kids leave home.

We wake up one day and realize our lives are half over and we still have no clue how to be happy within ourselves. It's not hard to change that if we pay attention. Instead of leaning on others, let us learn to be emotionally self-sufficient in the first place so there's no sense of losing part of ourselves when things change in life, as they always do.

Learning to be All One, Not Alone

As far as how to implement these ideas, a lot depends upon your current stage of life and your relationship status. If you are fortunate enough to be reading this as a young woman, about to leave your childhood home and head off to college or your own apartment, I encourage you to give a lot of thought to what kind of life you want. First and foremost, don't go straight from your father's direction to a husband's direction. You are in control and to hand that over to someone else never creates a healthy or positive situation. You need some time in the Soul Kitchen to perfect your recipe and bake your own cake before 'hooking up' with someone else. Stand on your own two feet and you will be a much more valuable partner. I have learned this the hard way.

Learn to be comfortable with yourself. Meditate, read, spend time in quiet thought, and build your self-confidence. You may want someone for companionship, sex, a dance partner, or to look good socially, but want is different from need.

Need infers desperation and there should never be desperation to be with someone else. Know yourself, love yourself, and enjoy your own company. Only then are you ready to share your life with someone else on anything but a superficial or casual basis. If you discover you only want to please him/her without an equal exchange of effort, you must re-evaluate your relationship and your recipe contents.

Ask yourself:

"Does this relationship feel balanced?"

If the answer is no, then you must change your ingredients. When we are in the needy column of life, we tend to over love or spoil our partner in an effort to make them happy. This must be recognized as overcompensation and nipped in the bud immediately as this type of behavior only leads to the loss and hurt that is inevitable with such a path. It's okay to want to please your partner; however it is imperative your partner also please you. An unbalanced cake tips over easily and a mess ensues.

Expect anyone you date, any serious companion or candidate for a permanent place in your life, to appreciate you for who you are, and not expect you to fade into the shadows of their spotlight. That doesn't mean you can't go along with his/her wishes or enjoy events and gatherings that person enjoys. It just means that you should expect them to value your interests as well and enjoy things you like. It must be a two-way street, not a cul de sac.

The point is, if your sweet life cake is delicious and fully baked, it can stand alone. The relationship, or frosting, is extra special but entirely optional! Being able to stand alone is not selfish, it is self-interested – a huge difference. Ever heard the expression 'if you don't love yourself, no one else will either'? It is a cliché, but very true. Selfishness is indulgent without creating something good or lasting. Self-interested means taking actions that are in your long term best interest. It has no negative connotations, instead it shows you are actively creating the life you want.

Being a Cupcake in a Cookie Cutter World

This is a couples world no doubt; people who choose to be single, or women who choose not to have children, are looked at skeptically. What's wrong with her? Everyone is expected to 'follow the norm' and if you're not married, you're supposed to be searching for a husband. Anything else, any other lifestyle, is often viewed as abnormal, perhaps even sad or pathetic. This prejudice can affect your career path and your social standing, which is unfortunate.

No matter what anyone else thinks, I know that it can be lots of fun to be single and I enjoy it very much. You get to do what you want, when you want. No one else's ridiculous rules or judgments to worry about. No annoying discussions about what to have for dinner. No eating meat and potatoes when you'd rather have a big crispy salad with apples and walnuts. You can go to bed when you like, and get up when you like. Weekends can be spent foraging for antiques or trying on clothes too expensive to buy. And best of all: you get possession of the remote control and the ability to watch chick flicks or the History Channel without an argument!

I never realized the prejudice single people face until I stayed single for more than a year without dating and started getting asked by friends if I was gay and not telling anyone. Why would someone think that way? It's just society's way of keeping us inside the predetermined box. I finally refused to play their game; you should too!

Often the questions and comments from others affect you when you choose to be single and I convey this as a warning that you must protect your newfound identity from being worn away by such prejudice.

This is one example from my own experience:

I am a real estate agent and once had a family come late in the day to view my showcased home.

As I was telling them all about the property, the wife said to me:

"We are sorry to come so late. We don't want to keep you from anything."

I replied, "That's okay, I'm single and I don't have any other plans for tonight." Obviously feeling sorry for me, she said, *"Oh, I am so sorry."*

With common sensibilities like hers, it is no wonder we feel we have to have a relationship to 'complete' us. Years of conditioning have brainwashed the majority of the human race to think that living single is somehow living a life that is 'less than'.

I smiled and assured her that touring beautiful model homes was my idea of a "fun evening" as she argued with her husband about the size of the home they should buy, and screamed at her children for running through the house, I bet she envied me a little!

Being Single Can Create
Some Social Awkwardness

I have noticed it is very difficult for some of my female friends to associate with me on a regular basis without their significant other having an issue with it. For some reason, a few men sometimes perceive a single woman as the leader of the 'She Woman, Man Haters Club,' which could not be further from the truth. The same is true of women who don't want their husbands to hang around their single male friends because they might 'lead them astray.' It is nothing more than insecurity. You can't make someone do what they don't want to nor can you keep them from cheating by monitoring their friends!

In my case, I can honestly admit that I love men! I love the idea of being with that special someone and having my life work in harmony with another. But the sad fact is that some married people act like their spouse having a single friend is detrimental to the marriage and so, I have lost some friends that I was quite close to as a married person. Now that I am single, they have made it known that I make them uncomfortable.

I have other friends with supportive spouses who are fine with my new single status and those friendships have endured. It's only the insecure partners who become very possessive. They are afraid their spouse may find some independence and truly see them for who they really are. This is a whole other topic that is supported by many books so we won't tackle it here. Just know that this could happen and you should prepare yourself by knowing that this circumstance has no bearing on you nor is it any sort of indictment against you because you decided to take control of your life. This is about the insecurity of others and there is nothing you can do about that so let it roll off your back and keep looking forward.

So secure am I in my own value, that on a recent Valentine's Day, I actively chose not to have a date and I went to a great, fancy restaurant. Yes, all alone. I ordered a glass of nice wine, had a great meal, and ignored the curious looks from other patrons, mostly couples. What I knew and they didn't was that I was doing exactly what I wanted to do, and I did not have to pretend to be enjoying the company of someone just for the sake of a date, or a great meal - which was probably not the case for many of those other restaurant patrons who looked down their nose at me! I loved it. Try it sometime. All One can be very empowering.

Does Size (or Age) Matter?

There are many preconceived societal notions that you may or may not have to deal with on occasion and these norms are as detrimental and sexist to men as they are to women. But the fact is that I have gotten more of these notions from women than I have from men. Ladies, we are often our own worst enemies by perpetuating these antiquated ideas via our girlfriends and daughters.

They include:

* *The man must be taller than the woman.*
* *The man must be older than the woman.*
* *The man must make more money than the woman*

  * *People should marry within their race.*

  * *People should marry within their religion.*

Most of these old-fashioned and misplaced notions have been debunked, thanks to the high visibility of successful couples who cross all the old boundaries and have flaunted the norm. This has served to increase the menu from which we get to choose our relationships. Granted, mixed race couples or oddly-sized couples might still get some sneaky looks in some environments, but so what? It's all about your cake and what flavor of frosting you choose. Even if you are a mature, well-aged rum cake, you are free to choose a sweet fresh German chocolate icing.

I say:

"Your wish is the command!"

Remember: There is no real 'normal.' There is just a collection of behaviors we have been taught to accept as normal, even if it is not reality. There are young people who are mature, and older people who are immature. Take the time to weed out the emotionally over-ripe and the too green, but be sure you take full advantage of the whole menu when considering any relationship. The selection has never been more vast.

That doesn't mean you shouldn't be selective and prudent in whom you pick. Often, someone just out of a serious relationship is quite vulnerable and not really ready to wholly be with someone else. You have to be strong enough to say no for their sake, and for yours.

Think about this for a second. When someone is hurting, they cannot be whole. If you are hurting and the other person is hurting, how can that be anything solid on which to build a strong foundation? I know the dangers of rebound relationships first hand, and am guilty of this desperate need to grab onto the first life raft that floats by. Once you have put some muscle into your self-esteem, you will be strong enough to resist.

I jumped into my second marriage without taking the proper time to heal from the damage inflicted by my first one. To make matters worse, he was recovering from a failed marriage too. We were like two accident victims, one with a broken left leg and the other with a broken right leg, leaning on each other to hobble down the road. We were both so incomplete, neither of us needed what we thought we wanted, which was simply to be a family again. To have someone to love and be with forever. A noble goal for sure, but not a successful strategy for long-term happiness. Give yourself, or your possible partner, time to fully heal before trying to become a couple.

I didn't do that. So after two years of living together, we tied the knot. I thought, If this doesn't work, and it probably won't, we can divorce. What the heck? Talk about a flashback! On some level, I knew it was happening again, but the fear of facing the inevitable, another failed relationship, lurked in the back of my mind so strongly I was willing to risk anything for a shot at being a wife in a stable home. What I found was that he and I were so broken from our first tries, and without proper time alone, it was inevitable our relationship would fail.

Over time, we both healed from the past hurts as our marriage progressed, however we also realized we had little else in common. We both worked hard in the beginning trying to make each other happy, only to realize neither of us wanted the same things out of life. When it was all said and done, the whole failed eight month debacle could have been avoided had we taken the time to be friends first and figure out that we were not equally yoked. Trying to blend the wrong ingredients at the wrong time just leads to, well, a hot mess. Because I still wasn't sure of the problem, I repeated the cycle for the next eight years, hurting myself and others along the way until I finally said enough is enough. It had to stop.

As you can see, for me it wasn't a fast or easy process to discover these truths that I'm sharing with you, but I am doing so in the hope that you learn faster and with much less heartache than I did. It took the better part of three decades for me to realize my own patterns and discover the reason behind those behaviors so I could change them.

You have the opportunity to right now start your own evaluation process and get on the road to your own happiness, perhaps sparing you a lifetime of disappointment and pain. I encourage you to take a deep breath and plunge right in. Jump into the deep end of the pool and swim toward the new you. Allow yourself the opportunity to step out clean and uncluttered on the other side and create a beautiful, rewarding and connected life.

> *Happiness and love are just a choice away.*
> *~ Leo F. Buscaglia*

Cake: Sherry Wilsher

An Affirmation for Choosing your Style:

I am beautiful and all of my choices allow
my confidence to grow.
My choice of style is unique to me,
for which I am happy

Exercise #3:

Think about the various times that people have judged you or made you feel incomplete, whether that was in reference to a relationship, financially, as a parent, or in any other way. Write down those comments that ate away at your self esteem. Now think of positive ways to respond to those old outdated ideas of what you should be that are based on someone else's ideas rather than your own happiness. Write your own affirmations that allow you to revel in your choices and your new confident life.

*The Lord doesn't see things the way
you see them. People judge
by outward appearance,
but the Lord looks at the heart.*
~ 1 Samuel 16:7

Pound Cake

Making a Better Batter;
Not Being Battered

*I*n designing a customized unique recipe for our own sweet life cake, we are going to mix our batter gently, carefully, forming it over time, not beat it to death. Nor are we going to allow anyone else, no matter how well meaning they are, to batter us with negativity or unwanted advice. I've heard some good friends call this 'muscling the universe' and that is exactly what it is. We think, we'll take a week or two and just whip ourselves into shape.

You may even be thinking:

"It took Sherry years to get her act together, but I'm sure I can get my life in order in a few months, tops!"

Not so fast super woman! There is a progression that has to take place and you can't just skip over the hard stuff, because I know you want to, so did I! But it only lead me to another eight years of discovery, so I wouldn't recommend the shortcuts because they aren't short at all.

As you start to create your own sweet life, you may have to scrap that old recipe, the one with lumps and too much starch or sugar. This new batter will be full of flavor and nutrition but it will require a lot of introspection and self discovery. It will be both sweet and savory, equal parts pleasurable and fulfilling. The best of both worlds!

To make sure your cake is right for you, you must sift through all the possible ingredients, being very choosy and selective. Only the best will do. Ingredients include all of the elements of life: job, lover, friends, family, wardrobe, makeup, hairstyle, car, entertainment and, hopefully, lots of sprinkles for fun.

Fast food off-the-shelf cake won't do, even though we humans do tend to get lazy and will grab what's handy. We are all guilty of this from time to time some more than others, depending upon our upbringing.

Let's think of our minds as brownies packed with dense, rich gooey goodness. When we're born, our mental recipes are packed with ingredients, some of them offering potential for tremendous success and greatness; others lurk deep in the batter and wait to sprout doubt, indecision, self-hatred, and poor self-image. Those negative ones were the ingredients that poured from my mind, as that was what was recognized and ingrained by my family environment. Maybe you can relate, or maybe you were one of the fortunate who had parental chefs that baked gentleness and nurtured the seeds of talent. If so, you are quite lucky indeed, but that wasn't the case at my house.

* *I was told that I wasn't pretty.*

* *I was warned not to get fat, as obesity ran in the family.*

* *"You will always need to wear makeup," I was advised.*

* *"Why are you always thinking about getting rich? You never will be"*
* *"Why do you always want to be something you're not?"*
* *"Live simple and cheap," I was told.*
* *Later it became, "He is out of your league. You are not pretty enough (or smart enough, or good enough) to marry someone like him."*

No Wonder My Poorly Constructed
Recipe Didn't Taste good!

What could flourish under those harsh conditions? What kind of tasty cake could emerge from a batter so rudely pounded? I am living proof, however, that you can overcome your upbringing, no matter how negative, unjust, or unfavorable to growth.

No matter what, I stuck to my decision to 'better' myself. Even at the very young age of five, I knew my life would be up to me. Instead of succumbing to the negative environment that surrounded me, I railed against it. I quietly rebelled. If someone told me to zig, I zagged, even without knowing why or what the consequence might be. I only knew I had to be different. Living any other way did not feel right to me. But then as I married and accepted my lot in life, I lost that drive and fell into a subservient mindset.

Strong female role models were hard to find when I was a child. All the women I encountered did not adhere to the strong independent role to which I was attracted. While I had (and still have) tremendous respect for those women to choose to make a career of homemaking and child rearing, I firmly believe they should retain their individuality and not melt into their partner or be treated as the family maid.

Back then, most of the women I knew seemed to have settled into a life of being a supportive companion, one for whom the husband would supply financial support in exchange for an orderly and well-managed household and sex on demand. It was a life that appealed to me as the way life should be, however I noticed that nearly every one of these relationships ended in divorce. Ultimately men lost interest in their housewives and the solid, if boring stability they represented.

The women also resented being taken for granted and resented that they were not allowed to flourish or pursue career dreams. Then the female, who had been taken care of, was either forced into getting a job or found themselves on the look-out for another man to fill the provider role for them. None the less, I wasn't going to allow myself to be in this type of situation. I always wanted to make sure I could pay my way, no matter what, even though I could not have verbalized it at the time. To me it represented freedom, because I just didn't see anyone I wanted to be like.

Successful women didn't exist in my day-to-day world growing up. I saw them only on television and an occasional teacher would become a bright spot in my life and I admired the ones who were the happiest. I became a huge fan of the sitcoms, nightly news shows, and eventually evolved to mimicking the anchor ladies on the nightly news for my beauty tips. I loved the stylish ways they wore their hair, they always looked so put together and beautifully made up. That was what I wanted.

Eventually, I found my way through trial and error (who knew that things looked differently on TV than they did in daylight, or under fluorescent light?) to my 'signature look.' Now, today, I am who I am for me. I dress and wear makeup according to my own style and what I find fun and attractive. I wear or not wear, do or not do, anything for anyone but myself. Age appropriate clothing, not always. Bling? Yes, please... Selfish? Nah, Just Sherry!

Trust yourself.

Actor and writer Steve Martin once said:

"For a while after 'The Jerk' (movie) I had a feeling of failure. I was a little scared. First people discover you and they love you. You get big and then you fail. And people are glad that you fail. But I've always come back and I've started to trust myself."

I love buying myself stylish or pretty things and trying out new cosmetics, clothing, and styles. Yes, I am living the way I have always wanted. I do what I want when I want, wear what I want when I want, say what I want when I want, and I like this real me. I encourage you to try it. Be yourself. God designed you and gave you incredible gifts. Develop them, enjoy them, and allow them to flourish. You will be ever so much happier than when you are hell bent on trying to please others. Believe it or not, you will please more people by being yourself than you will by trying to please them. What people who love you want is a happy, healthy you, and as for those who don't love you? Who cares? They are too self-absorbed for your actions to make any difference anyway.

I know all those negative statements that I allowed to hold me back throughout my life, all those cakes that fell flat, were not intended to destroy me. Unfortunately, they were almost always well intentioned. They were somehow thought of as 'protection' from failing and being hurt or disappointed. After all, if you sit at home in a ratty house dress, your hair all greasy, with no make-up on, nothing bad will happen to you. But neither will anything good. You will be bored, but you won't be harmed. By aiming low, or not aiming at all, you can't miss. I found out, though, that the higher I climbed, the better the view became. It was so incredible in fact that the possibility of failing paled in comparison to the endless opportunities I still discover daily. After all, William Faulkner considered himself a 'failed poet.'

Try It on for Size . . .

As women, we love to 'window shop,' and we understand that just because we want to try something on doesn't mean we want to buy it. I can only imagine what my closet would look like if I bought everything that I oohed and awed over while window-shopping. The same goes for finding a partner. It's okay to be choosey with whom you spend most of your time. If it doesn't fit, don't buy it. It's okay to say 'No thank you!' You have never invested too much time to step away nor are you ever obligated to anyone. Far too often we fall prey to the notion that if we 'date' or 'sleep' with someone, we are morally obligated to stay in the relationship or even marry them. Elizabeth Taylor explained to a reporter once why she had been married so many times. "I was a good girl," she said. "I wasn't about to sleep with someone un-less I was married to them." This can be a tragic and hurtful way to look at relationships. Better to exercise good judgment before hand, then end up married and divorced repeatedly.

Sticks and Stones . . .

For goodness sake, do not worry about labels or being called names. Envy goes by many names, sometimes even 'friend.' When creating your best batter, be selective, choose the very best ingredients you can find. Never settle for less than the best. Do your homework, step back a bit and take a rational, logical well thought out approach.

Always ask yourself:

"Is this a decision I can live with for many years to come?"

Our emotional side often pushes us to think in terms of :

"I don't want to lose this relationship"

But our 'dry' unemotional side might say:

"If you lose him, there's another one around the corner."

The different parts of your life - family, professional or business, social, spiritual - all need to be considered individually and then objectively as a whole batter when making any major life change. Make sure each part is taken into account when you're writing your best life recipe. Avoid 'paralysis through analysis' by over-thinking everything, but do take the necessary time to consider all the implications of your decision.

Once you decide on a course of action, discipline yourself to give it plenty of time to play out. Continuously opening the oven to check on your cake, or second guessing yourself, will cause it to fall!

> *I believe that man will not merely endure. He will prevail. He is immortal, not because he alone among creatures has an inexhaustible voice, but because he has a soul, a spirit capable of compassion and sacrifice and endurance.*
> *~ William Faulkner*

An Affirmation for Making

a Better Batter:

Today I choose the best ingredients for my life.
My choices are always to my benefit and my
happiness is a result of my decisions.

Exercise #4:

Think about the examples of people and the way they lived that you had in your own life. Did you see those whom you would like to emulate? If so, think about the qualities they had that you wanted in your own life. Write those down. Now think about the ways you can start working toward these attributes.

*Don't worry so much about
your self-esteem. Worry more
about your character.
Integrity is its own reward.
~ Laura Schlessinger*

5

Sponge Cake

Soaking Up Self-Confidence

*N*ow is the time for you to start choosing your own ingredients and building a life you deserve. You can think of this first step like baking up a sponge cake that will soak up lots of good things. Things that will boost your self-confidence and enable you to stand firmly on your own two feet.

Fall in Love – With Yourself! Your Real Self!

Deciding on the Right Ingredients

Remember, no one ingredient can make the cake by itself, it takes the right recipe of sweet and savory spices to bake up a delicacy. It's all about preferences, priorities, geographic location, lifestyle, work, church or spiritual home, residence, and much more. In this process, you should try very hard to determine your life's purpose. We are all here for a reason. No one can do this for you, and you should not allow anyone else to sway you away from your true purpose. It is perfectly acceptable, however, to look at the successful recipes baked up by others you admire. See what made their lives successful because there may be ingredients you can borrow.

These icons may even be members of your own family or church, folks you know at work, or parents of friends. I recommend you read lots of books, study, and soak up knowledge about what it takes to make a successful relationship and add to the various areas of your life. This is extremely important, so you'll need to invest some time and effort. Nothing worth having is going to come easy. No short cuts here!

Self-Confidence, Self-Esteem:
The Buzz Words We've all Heard...

I remember the first time I ever heard the word, 'self-esteem.' I had no clue what it even meant. I think I was in seventh grade. For awhile, the parenting community was all about building kids' self-esteem but most of it was superficial and amounted to letting them get away with anything. Obviously, I was lacking in the self-esteem department and did not even realize it until much later in life.

My hunger for change as a youngster was in part due to this lack of self-esteem and stemmed from being lead to believe I would never be good enough for what I desired.

Self-esteem really is the confidence to trust yourself and your choices. If you ask most people if they have self-esteem they will say yes, because it is hard to recognize that you may be lacking in that department. Many people think of the lack of self-esteem as something fear based. If someone is fearful then they will do what everyone else wants. But it is not that simple.

I can honestly say I wasn't afraid for my life or anything so dramatic, I just didn't value myself as equal to or worthy of the respect and dignity I gave to others. I seemed to free-fall my way through life without direction or aim, kind of like a pinball in a machine being bounced from experience to experience and dealing with things as they hit me the best way I knew how. Most of the time I chalked the bruising bumps up as an 'oops,' blamed my parents, and then was off in another direction to experience more of the same.

The cloak of self-esteem is something that we grow into over time, if we're lucky. I cannot pinpoint one event that made me more confident, it just gradually happened over time. Maybe it was blossoming all along, but I failed to notice its appearance until well down the road. Thousands of small things, insignificant on their own but powerful collectively, have been woven into my cloak of confidence. A little decision here that turned out well, a direction there that was rewarding, they all piled up in my heart and mind into a growing sense that I was worthy. The result is the way I walk, the way I talk, and the way I know without a doubt that I (and no one else) am in control of me. If you are searching, this is what I want to help you achieve – the perfect recipe for you. It may look different from what I experienced, but the result will be the same, a more confident you.

I recently had lunch with a lady with whom I do business. I do not know her well, however I do know she is a wonderful woman with a great attitude about life, her future is bright and promising. She told me during our conversation something about me was different than the women she normally meets, and she couldn't quite put her finger on it. "I am struggling with the word to use to describe you," she said. Eventually she came up with, "There is a certain presence about you." She then added, "When you enter a room, people take notice."

That affect is obviously only momentary, but she insisted that I 'capture' people. Her words made me feel so wonderful! I had been experiencing a strong calling to inspire others for such a long time and finally realized that is what I am supposed to be doing while I am here. That is my ultimate purpose, how wonderful to have finally found it!

With guidance from Above, I hope to inspire those who need a lift, for we all have our moments. Hopefully when I 'capture' someone's attention for a brief moment or for the span of time required to read this book, I can be a positive influence. As you find your purpose, I encourage you to build on the small triumphs and set aside the missteps and heartaches. As you dwell on those times that gave you a lift or small bit of inspiration, your true purpose will emerge.

Your Life's Purpose:
Thy Will be Done? Or My Will be Done?
Who's in Charge?

If you have never thought about having a purpose in life, I encourage you to take some time and think about it now. Everyone has a purpose. We all possess gifts, talents, abilities that are innate and unique to us. If you doubt me, think about the many savants, all of them severely challenged in various ways that keep them from participating in some of the simplest of daily functions of life that we take for granted. But these special, gifted individuals can play Chopin or look at a jar of jellybeans and know exactly how many are inside. There is an old Southern expression for this: God doesn't make any junk.

I don't mean to imply that every person is wonderful. Of course, that's not true. Evil does live among us, and many make the choice to turn their gifts into tools for wrongdoing. Because their ultimate purpose for good was not developed or realized does not mean it never existed. Once you define your life's purpose, your reason for being here, you are well on your way to baking up a sponge cake filled with self-confidence and determination.

Some Action Steps for Baking Up Your Life's Purpose:

1. Be present.

Live in the moment. That means to let yesterday go, and not worry about tomorrow. Keep a journal of good things and make a note every day of those little special things – a butterfly, a cloud shape, the sighting of an eagle, or a hug from a friend that gives you a little lift or inspiration. Re-read these daily or weekly, especially if you are having a rough time. It is human nature to exaggerate the bad and discount the good that happens to us each day. By spending some time reminding yourself of all the good, it lessens the hold of the negative events or comments you may hear during the course of your day.

2. Study and learn something new every day.

Ask questions, seek answers, be curious, and strive to keep your mind active and engaged. This doesn't necessarily mean keeping your nose in a book if that doesn't appeal to you. Go out and experience life. Maybe you attend a local street fair with various ethnic cuisines you've never tried. Take a continuing education class on photography, cake decorating, or even how to fly an airplane.

Think of all the things that you might like to experience before you die and start making a list. Travel, learn and most importantly, listen to yourself and what you really want. Do this for you, and you alone.

3. Find inspirational quotes.

Post them where you will see them. Listen to inspirational stories, see inspirational movies. Attend positive and uplifting conferences or seminars. This means lessening some of the negative garbage that you hear every day which can be a challenge, especially if it is coming from family or close friends. You have the choice to limit your time with them for a while until you are in a more positive space. You can be 'busy' or simply less available. Make room for you to get positive and learn to protect that budding confidence from the rest of the world.

4. Watch children at play.

Strive to recapture the free spirit and joy of your youth. If you didn't have a happy childhood, have one now. If you don't have children to observe, go to the pet store and watch the puppies play. Experience the new and exciting world from their eyes and remember the excitement that once came from small experiences. Allow yourself to be silly. If this means a stint of air guitar to your favorite Ozzy tune, then go for it and don't hold back!

5. Be a leader.

Don't wait for others to solve problems or offer a helping hand. Be the change you want to see in the world. I have some friends who live in Amarillo and one day they read in the newspaper that sixty four percent of the school children in their town qualify for food assistance and face some level of hunger. They decided to help a small program that gives elementary school children a backpack full of snacks each Friday to tide them over until they can once again eat at school the next week. Don't wait for someone else, just see what needs to be done and do it. You can help a neighbor or simply help yourself. Ladies stop with the 'honey-do' list and pick up a hammer! Men, turn on the Food Network and learn to make your own meatloaf. It may sound small, but there is a great feeling of accomplishment when you learn how to fix your own fence or replace a tail light in your car all by yourself. Or even bake your first turkey - which by the way I have yet to do.

6. Be healthy.

Eat a nutritious and healthful diet, get fresh air every day, and exercise. Taking a walk after a rough day can change your mental attitude and refresh your spirit. It's almost like a load is lifted off your shoulders and the problems seem much smaller. We all say we want to eat better, but live hopped up on caffeine and junk food. This is not about weight, although it certainly contributes to weight gain, it is more about feeling good and not being too tired to think about change.

Change takes effort and if you are getting even a little exercise, eating better and getting enough sleep you are less likely to be stressed out and overwhelmed. Sleep deprivation, especially for young parents, can cause tiny issues to spiral out of control. Keep these in check by taking better care of yourself.

Women, perhaps because we are the Mothers – the procreators – we tend to try to be more selfless and spend the majority of our time nurturing others. We support, organize, transport, shop, cook, do laundry, provide affection, all in an effort to make others happy and see that things run smoothly. Those are great qualities, but very often, we forget to nurture ourselves. We are often taught from infancy that self-love is narcissism and selfish. It is ego driven. But that is simply not true.

Remember how on the airplane the flight attendant says to first put the oxygen mask on yourself in an emergency, and then help others? We must be healthy mentally, emotionally, and physically in order to honor our creation and in order to care for others. When you are stressed out and overwhelmed you are more temperamental and angry. You get frustrated easier and those around you bear the brunt of your emotions. That is not fair to you or them.

If Mama Ain't Happy,
Ain't Nobody Happy

How you perceive yourself is much more important than how others perceive you, because a positive self-image leads to a positive reflective image. There are some relatively easy ways to give yourself an image boost, without spending thousands with a therapist or a plastic surgeon.

Work out or exercise every day, even if it's just taking the stairs at work or walking around the block at lunch. Do something physical, preferably outside. You will be amazed at how uplifting and energy boosting physical activity can be. Warning: it will become addictive. You will look and feel so much better you may invest in workout equipment and workout clothes.

Walk briskly, head and shoulders up, with a purposeful stride breathe deeply and re-energize yourself.

Dress nicely, even when just running errands. Pay attention to grooming even when it doesn't matter. It will matter to your ego, especially when you get a great compliment or catch a glimpse of your image in a store window. "Wow, who is that great looking babe? Oh, it's me!" This thought might make you giggle, or even wonder if it's pure conceit, but thinking well of yourself is not egotistical. Remember the cliché from earlier? If you don't love yourself, who will?

A friend of mine asked me once, "How come you always seem to have it together? You are always the right tanned color, your hair looks fab, and your nails are manicured, even pedicured!"

I told her that I keep the mind set, if someone were to call and say, "I have a great vacation planned to the Mediterranean and my friend can't go. Can you take her place?" I'd like to be able to say, "Of course!" (That did happen, by the way.) I don't want to have to scurry around trying to lose weight, get a haircut, and pull it together to feel and look good on the vacation. I can just be me because this is the real me!

Isn't it funny how most of us go into autopilot mode and become lazy and lifeless when we lose sight of our life's purpose? We just cruise along in low gear. It's much easier to eat a bag of chips and watch TV than to run three miles on the treadmill, reciting affirmations that feed our precious minds and add sweetness to our lives. It takes effort to meditate, pray and connect to recharge our life battery. I do understand the temptation to 'cruise' but I'm here to tell you that the rewards of, as Emeril Lagasse would say, 'kicking it up a notch' are really worth it. We can all remember a time when we went to the grocery store and ran into that old high school flame who looked hotter than ever while you were styling baggy sweatpants, a ponytail and no makeup. They probably didn't think much about it but it sticks with you for years and you are embarrassed that you got caught 'letting yourself go.' This doesn't have to be you anymore.

I have made the decision that I must commit to be the best I can be for myself on a daily basis. I'm not doing it for anyone else, just myself. This mindset has made my walk so much easier. From choosing the proper foods to eat, to making happy conversation with my friends and family, doing an hour of cardio exercise, and even enjoying the occasional dessert, I live my life on purpose! That means nothing is accidental; everything I do, every choice I make, is with a purpose in mind.

What's the Purpose?

The Sweet Life, of Course!

Thank someone. Be thankful and fill yourself with gratitude. Don't wait for the third Thursday in November; do it every day. Even setting a specific time each day to say thanks for all your blessings is a great idea. No matter what is going wrong in your life, there are always things to be grateful for. Look for them and acknowledge them. As we will see later in our discussion of the Laws of Attraction, you will soon see that the more things you say thanks for, the more good things will come your way.

Display positive, open, body language. Arms crossed over your chest, for example, present a barrier. Keep your head up, smile often, be energetic. When you are insecure or hurt we tend to close ourselves off from others or give off those 'don't talk to me' vibes. These don't help you get to a better place, so make a conscious choice to be friendly and smile even when you might not feel like it. Eventually you will be happy, but you have to make the conscious choice to be happy before it can happen. If you keep waiting on someone to come along and 'make' you happy, it's going to be a long wait.

Read and listen to motivational teachers. We already talked about this a little bit, but this goes deeper than daily affirmations. Post positive messages where you will see them frequently, and listen to confidence-building CDs or podcasts in your car. That's a much better investment in your time than listening to shock jocks or depressing newscasts. There are many teachers around the world who can offer insight and inspiration on your journey. One that speaks to you might not speak to me and visa versa so try out a few and see which ones seem to touch you. It's easy to lose motivation and very hard to get it back or maintain it on a continual basis so pay attention to this aspect of your life and choose to motivate yourself because like practicing happiness, no one can do it for you.

Defend and compliment others as often as possible. Be a positive influence on those around you. This has nothing to do with if they deserve it or if they have done something for you. Each day you meet people during the course of daily life that you probably don't even notice. The guy on the corner that you buy your coffee from or the chef at your favorite sushi restaurant that makes your favorite tuna roll. What about the person standing in line behind you that is wearing a really beautiful tie or pair of shoes? It is okay to give random strangers a compliment. It makes everyone smile and this world can use more of them, so could you. It can take a little time to get used to doing this, especially if you have been out of practice so you can start with picking just one person each day to compliment. Maybe it's something small or something you've wanted to say for years, but it will be meaningful to you both so don't wait.

Put yourself forward and never cower against a wall or in the back row. You are smart, confident, and you have something to offer any gathering. When it's appropriate, or when you have something to add to the conversation, speak up. Don't be a wallflower. Once you get the hang of this, the positive effect will feed upon itself and you will gain tremendous self-confidence as people start responding to you and to your intellect. I sometimes say the silliest things and often make others laugh, when that may have not been what I was going for, but it is simply the way I am.

Yes, I have often kept my mouth shut when I could have spoken up. Now, when I have the chance, I will say just about anything. Shocking answers to questions seem to be my nature, so I just go with what I feel at any given time. You, too, should trust your instincts and be yourself.

Join a networking organization. I belong to a couple of them. One of them is the E-Woman Network, a powerful organization of women supporting women. A special thank you to our Houston's Executive Manager, Terri Craig, for being such a strong supporter of this book, as well as encouraging women to follow their life's passions and supporting them in such an inspiring way. You may join a church group, the Rotary club or any number of organizations that allow you to get out there and mix and mingle with colleagues and new friends.

Connecting with others gives you a bigger support system and decreases feelings of loneliness as you make new connections and spend time with new and varied people.

Worry less about yourself, and focus more on others. Now this may seem contradictory, because I've been telling you to focus on yourself. True, you should focus on improving yourself and growing as a person, but that doesn't mean to become self-absorbed in a negative way. Stop dwelling on your own problems and self-pity. There is a whole big world out there with much bigger issues, and they could use your help!

Volunteer, contribute, and do something for someone else. As you help others and stop allowing your mind to dwell on the bad in your life, it becomes less and less of a force to deal with. It will allow you to go from being a drama queen to a solid, caring person who delights in the success of others.

Loveable You

Falling in love with 'you' does not refer to narcissism. Narcissus was a legendary Greek figure who saw his own reflection in the clear waters of a pool and fell in love with his own image, which eventually led to his destruction. Of course, the story has a moral about getting too wrapped up in the trappings of the physical body and how we identify with it, which can lead to our own issues and become a tragic flaw.

In truth, you are so much more than is reflected in a mirror. That's not to say you shouldn't honor the body temple and make yourself as healthy and attractive looking as possible. Make the best of it by all means, but when I talk about loving yourself, I mean learning to accept and revel in the wonder that you are, especially as a woman.

We have very special physical attributes given to us by our Creator and we should appreciate them. We are built to procreate humankind and to nurture infants. That is a special gift and talent for sure.

When you are a young person growing up with self-doubt, it is easy to feel like anyone who would like you had to have something wrong with them. Until a few years ago, this is how I felt about anyone who showed interest in me, and it was like the ol saying Groucho Marx coined and later Woody Allen used in the Annie Hall movie:

*"Why would I want to belong to a club
that would have me as a member?"*.

That is exactly how I felt about anyone who loved me. This mindset kept me from truly loving another with a deep caring love and maintained my place in the "searching" mode for happiness. Until I fell in love with me, I had no clue how to truly love another.

We get into relationships, be they with friends, lovers, children and other family members. Their needs are always put before our own. It is considered true if we take care of ourselves first, we are then much better caretakers of those who 'need us.'

Good relationships support each other in individual growth and enhances the relationship overall. Why do so many people, especially women, fall into the trap of neglecting themselves? While we won't solve the question here, I do urge you to prioritize your physical, mental, and spiritual health. This will help you be successful in your relationships, your career and most importantly, your life.

Believe you can and you're are half way there.
~ Theordore Roosevelt

Cake: Sherry Wilsher

An Affirmation for Soaking
up Self-Confidence:

*Today I choose the best ingredients for my life.
My choices are always to my benefit and my
happiness is a result of my decisions.*

Exercise #5:

Search out teachers and those who inspire you. Attend
seminars or read books that allow you to grow spiritually
and emotionally. Make a list of the issues in your life you
would like to move forward on, or discover more about,
and then search out those answers.

*NOTES:

We will discover the nature of our particular genius when we stop trying to conform to our own or to other peoples' models, learn to be ourselves, and allow our natural channel to open.

~ Shakti Gawain

6

Carrot Cake

Getting and Staying Healthy,
Inside and Out

* *

Who knew something as nutritious as the carrot could be turned into such a tasty sweet cake? If you've ever had a delicious slice of carrot cake, you know this to be true. Likewise, zucchini bread is utterly delicious and tastes nothing like the vegetable.

To be our best selves, and to be able to stand strong against societal pressures. We must be physically as well as mentally fit. We have to each find our own perfect balance between sweet and savory in our lives.

In other words:

"A carrot cake a day keeps the doctor away".

From the Mouths of Babes

Christine Boss, Pharmacist, Personal Trainer and founder of Core Intervention, LLC is a well-known and highly respected personal training and health management expert located in Houston, Texas. She has graciously contributed the following information for getting and staying healthy (thus wealthy and wise!):

Ever wished you could be that person you've always pictured in your imagination? You know, that enviable person who people admire, the one who gets what they want in life, is confident, and seems to get all the breaks?

It is entirely possible when you do this ONE thing:

See yourself as that person.

Seeing is Believing

Self-image is one of the most powerful parts of our personality – a secret weapon - yet we were most likely not taught how to positively develop it either in school, by our parents, our friends, or even society. We've pretty much been left on our own to react to adversity and insults with strength, grace, and confidence OR buckle under the threat and retreat into weakness and submissiveness. Some become bullies themselves. Your self-image determines how you see yourself, how you feel about yourself, how you handle your life on a daily basis and under specific circumstances. It determines what you think your 'role' is in society and what you expect to receive in life.

It also determines where your 'comfort zone' is – the things you would and would not do. Those of us who buckled under childhood threats to our psyche set ourselves up for a stressful adulthood. When exposed to a similar insult, this triggers mental misery. When confronted with your personal item of conflict, you become uncomfortable and the ordeal creates a terrible feeling of helplessness usually causing you to stifle your emotions so you are able to 'suck it up.' This can make you prone to habitual gloominess, guilt, and worst of all, actual physical illness.

Many oncologists (cancer specialists) subscribe to the theory that our reactions to psychological stress can profoundly affect the outcome of treatment as well as cause the recurrence or growth surge of cancer cells. I have also found in my experience as a pharmacist and personal trainer that these same phenomena can manifest as diabetes, high blood pressure, and obesity.

Have you ever tried to set a goal larger than what you are currently used to, then quietly backed down, returning to your comfort zone and falling back into old habits without realizing it? That's because your self-image was regulating your success. You backed down because deep down inside, it didn't feel like something you would or could do. Supposed you were asked to go into a room full of strangers and introduce yourself to each and every one of them with a big smile, would you do it? Unless you thought of yourself as a naturally likeable, outgoing person, you probably wouldn't do it. The thought of it would probably make you nervous, maybe even nauseous. You would probably say something like, "No thanks, that's just not who I am." That is because that's who you think you are, or in this case, are not.

The things you attempt to do, the way you think people treat you, even the clothes you choose to wear, are all determined by the picture you have of yourself in your head. I have seen over and over again how personal training clients start out shy and introverted, then over a period of a few months, develop confidence and a totally different self-image emerges as they progress in their training. They learn to believe they are capable and prove to themselves that they can do things they never thought possible. If they believe that they can lift a ninety-pound barbell, they do. If they believe they can resist the piece of birthday cake at work, they do. They see themselves as who they want to be and then actually become that person. Physical training forces you to step out of your comfort zone and, yes, it is uncomfortable at first, but it creates a belief in yourself that is nothing short of miraculous. I have seen clients go from overweight to winning physique contests. I have seen clients eliminate their dependence on medications. They experience a freedom that they often can't adequately describe it is so profound.

Working as a personal trainer, I have helped clients understand they have control over three very important things that ultimately puts them in charge of their health and body shape. These things are the foods they eat, exercises they do, and the amount of rest/ relaxation they enjoy. The mastery of their bodies that clients experience for themselves translates into their personal lives and they are more confident and in control there as well. They realize they have a choice in how they choose to live their life. They can be rich or poor, thin or overweight, happy or depressed, outgoing or shy, smart or stupid, well dressed or slovenly. As exemplified in CAKE, they can choose to be a single layer cake, a cupcake, or a big confection with frosting!

My clients know there are "No rules...only choices." I have seen average people make extraordinary changes because of one thing: They changed their self-image. They learned how to believe in themselves through their success in the gym. They learned how to age gracefully. They replaced the refrigerator photo of the overweight sad person with someone who is healthy and happy, and that new picture implanted itself into the psyche.

Use the Buddy System

It would be very beneficial to find a solid and dependable work-out partner or a good, supportive personal trainer, because once you get control of your body, you are unstoppable in gaining control of your life.

It's a proven fact that you cannot rise above your self-image, you must change the self-image and give it an upgrade. Take control of yourself physically and you will succeed mentally.

I agree with Christine wholeheartedly. When I turned forty, I faced many issues. Several of which I have shared with you. I awoke one morning with the realization that I was getting older and my self-image was suffering along with my ability to know how to fix it. I figured that if I had a face lift, I would be transformed into the beauty I longed to be. So I consulted a couple of different plastic surgeons, both recommended 'the works,' which would have cost more than twenty-five thousand dollars. After sleeping on it and reading the materials associated with the procedure, I asked myself, "why do you feel you need this type of dramatic procedure?" The reality of the matter was, no matter how much I spent on refurbishing the chassis, I would still be the same on the inside. No amount of nipping and tucking would change my inner self. The old phrase, 'beauty from within' kept surfacing and after conversing with a friend, she suggested I hire a trainer and go that route.

So I Did

Cosmetic surgery is fine for some, it can be a wonderful boost to self esteem. But you have to do it for the right reasons and not just to cover up emotional issues. That's what I was doing, looking for a way to frost over the problem.

Again, had I gone that route at that time, I wouldn't have been any happier, so I'm glad I made the decision I did. That doesn't mean I won't seek a nip or tuck at some point, but if and when I do it will be for the right reasons, to enhance the real me, not cover it up.

Obsession is something else I've mentioned. Yes, you guessed it, I became addicted to exercise, clean eating, and the overall high that I achieved from feeling and looking years younger. I felt I had found the fountain of youth and I wasn't about to let it go or risk losing it by taking a day off from the gym.

As with anything, I have learned that through finding the proper balance, one can be incredibly physically fit and still have a life outside the gym. It is just one part of your life and important, but it must be balanced with other parts of life to become the perfect part of the whole of your life. It is your choice and decision to determine how much physical fitness you need to achieve a healthy self-image. That does not necessarily mean a perfect physique as defined by some anorexic supermodel, but it is all about the right physical and healthful well-being for you.

An individual's self-concept is the core
of his/her personality.
It affects every aspect of human behavior.
~Dr. Joyce Brother

An Affirmation for Getting
and Staying Healthy:

Today I choose health. The food I consume and choices I make regarding my physical and mental well-being are the best suited for my goals.

Exercise 6:

Keep notes for one week on what you eat, how much you exercise and how much sleep you get each night. Most of us eat much more than we think and exercise and sleep much less than we realize. After one week, review your results. Are you getting enough sleep? If you are getting less than 7-8 hours you may need more sleep! Are you exercising at all, or enough to feel good? If not, think of ways you can add small bits of exercise here and there. Commit this next week to think about the food you are eating before you just pop it into your mouth. Are there healthier choices? Am I eating because I'm hungry or bored? Are there emotions I'm hiding behind food?

*A person sooner or later discovers
that he/she is the master-gardener
of the soul, the director of life.*
~James Allen

Angel Food Cake

The Sweet/Heavenly
Law of Attraction

I discovered the Law of Attraction while reading *The Secret* by Rhonda Byrne, and my life was forever changed. I used the principles of this book and the Christian teachings I was raised with to create the best formula for me. This is one of several important books you will find in the **Refrences & Resources** page at the end of this book. Your goal in creating your sweet life is to increase the decibel level of the positive voices inside you to the point that they drown out external opinions and events. Firmly embrace the concept that you are in charge of your destiny. As James Allen said, you are the director in your 'life movie.'

This is a beautiful subject and there is no way I can do it justice in a single chapter. I encourage you to learn more about this and how it can expand and help fulfill your life. Once you see the simple message, you will start to see where the Law of Attraction has been present in all areas of your life.

If there is any moment in time I knew without a doubt I was the designer of my life, it was after I experienced my true awakening while studying about the Law of Attraction. Once I really understood it, I realized how empowered I was in my own life. With God as my source, I could create whatever I wanted. What a concept from what I had experienced as a child, where life was all about worry and how bad things were. All fear was released and I knew everything was going to be all right. It was a moment of clarity and self-empowerment and I will never forget it. I want that moment for you - that feeling of never having to depend on someone else for happiness, security, fulfillment, or satisfaction. I had myself to rely upon, and all the talents and abilities given to me by God, and that was more than enough. The Law of Attraction is actually very simple, yet the complexities of it are endless.

The law says that you control your future and your destiny. The past no longer matters. What you think about, and what you put your energy toward, materializes. After all, every single great invention or discovery began with a single thought. That's an amazing concept, so take a moment to really grasp that.

Thoughts lead to things and those things will manifest in your life. Thoughts lead to everything! Sub-conscious beliefs attract people, circumstances, and experiences into your life. When you think about that idea, it can put you off a little. After all, it doesn't feel like I attracted my failed marriage, but if I really think about it, I did. I knew it wasn't right, but went full steam ahead with it. I knew different. I stifled my own voice and crushed the power I had over my own life.

I realized through studying this law that I could change the way I thought and that my results would change – and did they ever! By dwelling on past hurts and perceived unfair acts of my parents, I robbed myself of my future. Since I could only think about everything that was wrong, I attracted negativity into my life. Once I released those thoughts and replaced them with the kind of life I wanted to live, my attitude, outlook and feeling about my life did a one-eighty. I had the power to change anything and was almost giddy with a kind of new found hope my future would be that different life I sought to lead when I was only five.

I started by writing down my dreams for my future. Whether you write them down or record them, it is important to create a record of what you want. By doing this you are setting things in motion for the Universe/GOD to bring about the fulfillment of those desires.

As Mark Victor Hansen said:

"Put your future in good hands – your own."

Whatever you focus upon increases. If you repeatedly tell the Universe that you don't want car troubles, for example, what the Universe hears is 'car trouble' and believe me, that's what you'll get. It is essential to always form your thoughts, prayers, pleas, and goals in a positive format. 'I want' rather than 'I don't want'. Follow this up with being grateful for what you do have. Once you truly believe your dream or goal is possible, this is when the magic begins.

Close your eyes and imagine you have already achieved that desire. How does it feel? Do goose-bumps ripple across your arm? This kind of intense emotion is exactly what your dream needs to manifest. These little changes spawn a healthier belief system and allows bigger and sweeter wishes to be granted. Always expect the best and don't wait for the downside or for the other shoe to drop. It's a habit you have to create, but once this is achieved, your life will change.

Here are some important quotations to remember:

"Remember, whatever you focus upon, increases...When you focus on the things you need, you'll find those needs increasing. If you concentrate your thoughts on what you don't have, you will soon be concentrating on other things that you had forgotten you don't have-and feel worse! If you set your mind on loss, you are more likely to lose...But a grateful perspective brings happiness and abundance into a person's life."
~Andy Andrews

"Anything we focus on we do create. So if we're really angry, for instance, at a war that's going on, or strife, or suffering, we're adding our energy to it. We're pushing ourselves, and that only creates resistance."
~Hale Dwoskin

Are you skeptical? I was at first; the whole idea of a Law of Attraction seemed so simplistic and too good to be true. Let me put your doubts to rest.

The Law of Attraction is a complex and multi-faceted approach to life and an entire philosophy all on its own. While the idea may sound easy, implementing it takes time and focus. It's common to take one step forward and then two back as your comfort zone beckons you back.

It's easy to slide into your normal routine and old ways of thinking, but those ways did not produce happiness before, so why would you allow yourself to stay in that way of thinking? When you dwell on the past, you have a choice to instead focus on your new life.

I know without a doubt it's the way to the life of our dreams. *The Secret* teaches this, however deeper knowledge has to be acquired to really grasp it and that knowledge comes from studying, evaluating, spending time in prayer and meditation, and then acting - then doing it all over again. Our programming from generations of made up invented 'Societal Rules' have hindered the human mind from realizing what's readily available to us, what was intended from the beginning.

Thank God for Rhonda Byrne and her book, *The Secret*, which was my first real exposure to the 'Law of Attraction' and presented in a simple enough way for me to grasp. At the time I discovered this, I was so turned off by Religion that had the book mentioned anything about the subject, I would have put it down. However, after soaking up the message, I started to put two and two together and found my spirit leading and happiness prevailed. I know I have barely scratched the surface, but am well on the path to uncovering more of its nuances and to this day, I still hunger for more truths. That appetite for answers keeps me motivated, that is the Law in action!

Like attracts Like ...

Ever heard the expression, 'birds of a feather flock together'? That expression has long been used to describe the fact that people with similar characteristics attract one another. This is very true and we don't really notice it happening because it is taking place on a subconscious level. Not only does it happen with people, it happens with things and events in our lives. Have you ever heard the phrase, 'what you believe, you receive'? That is the Law of Attraction at work.

I know you've heard stories, too, about people who expressed an idea or desire and within a short time it came to be even though it was an extreme long shot. You probably dismissed them as coincidence. I think it's more like serendipity - a fortunate accident. Make no mistake, you do have some control over these 'accidents' in life and can even attract them to you.

If you start writing down all the coincidences in your life, you will be amazed. Think about the times you've run into an old friend you were just thinking about. How often has someone flashed into your mind only for the phone to ring and it be that exact person? When were you in the exact right place in time to meet someone who would change the course of your life? How many times have you been delayed only later to be spared being involved a horrific accident thanks to that delay? Many people also attribute these serendipitous events to 'an angel on their shoulder.' I certainly don't dismiss that either. We must keep out minds and hearts open to receiving whatever gifts the Universe has to send our way. Blessings and gifts may float by on a gentle wind and if we're not constantly alert, we will miss them forever.

Polar Opposites

Are you constantly irritated by the friends you have, the way your family behaves, your job, and your current life path? Those negative thoughts and feelings act as a barrier to the universal gifts previously mentioned. Negative thoughts are like a hard clear plastic shell or barrier that allows you to see what you want, but keeps you from touching it. If you have a hard shell of negativity surrounding you, how could you possibly experience the good .

You must stop dwelling on the negative. Look carefully at your overall view of life and examine what thoughts run across the bottom of your life screen like that never ending text scroll on TV. That steady stream of negativity saps your energy and acts as a shield warding off the good!

Opnions are hindering thoughts that attract the negatives. Harboring negative opinions on any subject is poison to your mind and must be eliminated. Do you sit with friends and pick apart co-workers? What they wear, how they talk, who they hang out with? Are you critical of every situation pointing out every bad possibility? Do you gossip and 'stir the pot' with people you know, then sit back and watch the fireworks?

This behavior is a habit formed over a lifetime, but with the decision to change, it can be overcome. It takes time and conscious effort to hold your tongue, and then to find something nice to say instead. Positivity is infectious and as you change, others around you will notice and not only like the change, but choose that change for themselves as well. Put the fragrant yeast of positivity into your life recipe and just watch it rise.

Negativity grows like mold on bread when people share their opinions. Not only is our environment poisoned, we've poisoned our family, friends, and co-workers. In turn, each of them in turn spread the toxic mold and you are now the source of lots of negative vibes floating around in the Universe. The negativity takes over like the plague and there's a muck of a situation that often results in harming another person, especially if the opinion gets back to them. Hurtful! Remember, this truth really applies to any subject: Negative opinions have to be pushed aside and not allowed to have a place in your mind - even for a second.

When I quit expressing my negative opinions, people started to think I didn't care about anything, but I do. I have occasional negative thoughts like everyone else, I just don't hold on to them as they do not serve me. The opinions I want to give my energy to are positive and can have a good influence on something or someone. If I don't have something positive to say, I keep my mouth shut. Believe me, no one really cares about your opinions, especially the negative ones. We all have them, but typically they are just noise that keeps drama in our lives and keeps our 'my life sucks' story going.

Gossip falls into this category. Gossip tends to be negative and never does anyone any good. It is nearly always someone's attempt to seem 'in the know.' If you find yourself chatting it up about another person, even if it's a seemingly harmless little story, slam the mental door and walk away. Believe me, it's not worth it. Something negative is always harmful. If you have something positive to say, say it directly to the person! The gossip habit is highly addictive and habit forming but it can be broken, it just requires a decision to be made and an ongoing conscious effort to change.

Yes, a decision seems simple, however the dramas our minds are intent on keeping us stagnant in life by making it seem fun, harmless, or nothing more than idle chit chat. It is anything but. You can choose to stop spreading the mold and instead start spreading sweet ingredients that uplift and encourage.

Ask, Believe, Receive

It really is that uncomplicated, however here's the catch: Belief lives in our subconscious mind! "Ahhh," you moan, "you didn't say that!"

The subconscious is where those automatic responses and habits reside. Once we figure out how to re-program this part of our minds, that is when the real magic begins. So, how does this happen? This is done primarily through daily positive affirmations. It must become part of your life, like breathing, so that you no longer have to think about being positive or attracting positive, it happens naturally.

You can think of it like riding a bike. It takes a lot of effort and trial and error, but eventually you get the hang of it. Once you do, you don't really even think about how to balance when you get on a bike, you just do it, even if it's been years. Your thoughts are the same way.

You can't just make a wish and watch it manifest itself, like tossing a coin in a fountain and finding a million dollars in your purse. Wouldn't we all love that? You could certainly do that – make that fanciful wish - but what about the other part of the equation? That part that says you must have an absolute belief in your ability to obtain your goal or desire. Even then, things don't create themselves in such a literal way. You may want to be a millionaire, but how that happens may take many twists and turns. You may find an advertisement for a job that eventually leads to your rise to CEO and the accomplishment of that goal. Or someone may offer to buy your property for a million dollars because of its location for future development. In other words, the Universe provides opportunity when you follow all of its laws. Most people fall down on the one hundred percent belief part, so when the opportunity comes along to give them what they desire, they don't recognize it as such or they second guess their own ability. They trip themselves up rather than believing.

I have learned over the years how to acquire anything I focus upon. There is, however, a process of growth my mind has had to experience in order to get to my prizes, my desires. It's sort of like piecing a jigsaw puzzle together without having the box lid that shows what the final result looks like. One tiny piece interlocks with another until eventually the full scene emerges. First, though, you will just see large swaths of colors, and shapes that don't make sense and don't connect. Finding the missing puzzle pieces and trying to figure out the big picture is part of life's challenge and what makes this journey so exciting, rewarding, and such a fun experience for us.

Another way to think about this process is to envision a road map with only the destination marked; no routes are visible. How far do you really want to go? How big is your dream? What stops and side trips will you make along the way? Will you take the wrong road? Stop? Go backward? Your mind is the only thing that can produce what you are after and only you determine your own route to get there. So, you think your dream is big? Maybe too big to be achieved? For you it may seem that way, for others, maybe not because they have already achieved it and moved on. It's true that some people go in a direct and short path to their dreams while others may wander around for years to get to the same goal.

Have you ever wondered why some folks are so successful and others, who are equally as talented and smart, cannot succeed? Well, it all goes back to that subconscious programming – their ingrained negativity. Our early life programming. This is especially of the negativity and low expectations often imposed on girls, which must be overcome to the point of total reprogramming sometimes.

What I have found to master this, and believe me, I am still on the learning side of it, is that: You simply must first and foremost, realize what you really want. Patience is required. However your desire must remain the constant in your mind. Deeply rooted to the point it becomes a destination. It will be an obsession, but a healthy positive obsession.

Keep in mind, desiring a certain person doesn't fit into this process. Humans are unique with desires and wills of their own. Our wishes are the 'feeling' we want to obtain when acquiring what we want. The feeling you are after will be achieved only when you let go of the exact one you are longing for and allow the right one into your life.

You want that big beautiful house on the corner because you believe with all your heart that it will keep you safe and secure. It will be your haven and your fortress to protect you against all that may be wrong in your world. Once you get that home, however, you discover its flaws. You are once again unhappy and dissatisfied and don't understand why. Perhaps your desire should have more specifically dealt with why you feel you need protection? Perhaps you need a home, not necessarily that home. Or worse yet, you kept phrasing your desire as a need for safety or protection and suddenly found yourself working in a condom factory! I'm joking, of course, but do you see my point? Your desire must be expressed specifically and in a positive framework. Be careful what you wish for.

A personal Story That May

Sound Familiar to You

I grew up with a co-dependent personality. It held me firmly in place without the courage to leave my unhappy and unsatisfying life situation without some sort of backup plan. Of course, like most women, my backup plan consisted of a man. I was not looking for anything in particular or even actively searching, I really wasn't. I never layed awake and daydreamed of finding a new love. I honestly never thought of it, at least not consciously. Somewhere in the depths of my subconscious, however, I must have had the wish for 'true love,' because one day, I saw him. He was someone I had known and worked with in the past, but had never paid much attention to. He flirted with me one day and the fire of passion was ignited. It was like a fresh log on a dying campfire. I knew he and I had something unique. Because of our previous casual workplace friendship, the basics were already established, so I felt safe.

He had been single for many years and I often wondered why, but hey, a challenge is always appealing to me, so I proceeded 'without' caution.

(Notice the tendency of going from one man to another)

Even though on some level I knew I needed *Sherry Time*, and needed to be independent for a while, I fell in love with this man and failed to act in my own best interest.

After only a few weeks with him, I started to see why he was single. Not that he had any glaring or obvious visible flaws, he just seemed unable to commit to anyone, even someone whom he cared deeply about. I did not understand this at all. He cared a great deal about me so what was his hesitation? He and I were addicted to each other, however, and could not leave it alone. I was willing to take whatever he was willing to give. Though mentally unhealthy and as disappointing as a cake without sugar, we had reached a point in our relationship where we were very okay with each other and understood the other's need to be together occasionally. Then one day without warning, he shut me out.

I was devastated, confused, blindsided, and could not understand this abrupt stop sign he had put between us. My heart shattered into a million pieces. I felt like I was falling off a cliff without a net. I was so emotionally out of control over this event that it consumed every fiber of my being. I went to counseling, however, decided he was crazy so I could let go. But I loved him anyway.

I tried to figure out everything I could think of because, for the first time I was truly facing the inevitable. Sherry alone. Oh, my goodness! How in the heck was I going to manage with no man in my life? Needless to say, the rejection from him devastated my weak self-esteem and it took months to regain any semblance of confidence. I slipped into a deep depression and felt very alone and like I wanted to die.

One day I woke up and asked God:

"Why? Why am I alone and feeling this way?"

His answer soft and calm, I felt these words wash over me:

"This is your wish."

The message continued:

"Sherry, you've known you need this in order to get to your ultimate destination in life. This is part of your journey so adapt to it, accept it for what it is, take it one day at a time, and one day it will all make sense."

As painful as that message was to hear, I had no choice but to take the advice from God, my Guide, whomever it was connecting with me in such a way. I felt peace for the first time in months.

About two months later, I heard my friend had been diagnosed with Stage IV esophageal cancer and his chances of survival were not very good. My beloved was about to face the inevitable death we will all one day face. He was going to move from this life to another. Was this the reason he had cut me out of his life? Preparing me to be without him? Forcing me to stand on my own two feet? If that was the case, he never articulated it, but I believe it to be true.

His battle with cancer raged and he swiftly lost the war. I knew he was very sick, but a part of me still hoped he would somehow pull off a miraculous recovery and we could be the couple he and I often talked about becoming. I had another reality check. For the first time I understood that just having the hope of once again being with the love of my life was keeping me from being independent and truly finding the real love of my life: *Me*.

The realization dawned that there would never be an 'us' and that image had to be removed from my wish list, leaving a blank space there that would have to be filled. I was also faced with figuring out why this man had been a relatively brief but very important part of my life. The puzzle piece he represented takes up a great portion of my life's picture and purpose. Remove that piece and what happens to the big picture of my life?

The precious and wonderful time with him, though short, woke up a part of me that I never knew existed. For it was he that made me feel beautiful again. Gave me the courage I needed to step out and claim the independence I craved. Finally, I am both alone and all one, and best of all, I am happy. Yes, I miss him, I grieve deeply for him, but I now choose to detach emotionally from the 'could have been' yet hold onto the gifts he gave me during our time together.

As I work hard to wean myself from my addiction to the feelings evoked by him, and my firm belief that through him I could find true and lasting happiness, I am learning day by day that I must now change the directions on my life map. I must set the destination as 'Love' and not a particular person. I must leave room for the Law of Attraction to work, and to attract the person who is right for me, and for whom I am the right person. It will happen, I'm sure of it. After all, it's the law and I am allowing!

A close girlfriend of mine has an ex – a long-term partner who believes that the only way to his happiness is to have her back, but unlike other desires, relationships are a two-way street. The man tells acquaintances that he will prove to her that he can be the man of her dreams if given another chance. He is convinced of his ability to do that. What he doesn't understand is that she does not love him the same way he loves her. There is no way on Earth he can change that with believing she will. We cannot wish someone to love us back the way we want them to, no matter how hard we try.

Remember how in junior high the big question was, "What can I do to make him like me?" The answer is: you can't. Not even with potions, black magic, wishing wells, Valentine cards, driving by his house a million times, or pretending to be something you're not. Oh, you can make someone spend time with you, or look at you, or even date you, but you can't make them love you. You should stop trying. Wish for love, not for that person.

When we figure out how to change the way we think and deliberately choose the thoughts that are beneficial and fuel those thoughts with passionate intention we develop the belief of what is truly possible. That is when we master our lives through the *Law of Attraction.*

I never knew this law until a few years ago, however I somehow managed to make it this far in life with something guiding me toward it. We all live by this law whether we understand it or not. The hunger for the truth and an open mind allowed me to attract it into my life. My mindset and my life is forever changed and I hope to bring that change into your life through this book.

The Message is Simple:

Like Attracts Like

It's really no more complicated than that, and without getting too deeply into religious beliefs, it is my personal conviction that Jesus Christ's beautiful message was just as simple and straight-forward: **Truth.**

He was the greatest teacher of love, and he taught this very message, but over the centuries, mankind has inexplicably complicated it by placing so many rules and regulations upon it (do this, don't do that), making it nearly impossible to fully 'get it.' The design of the Universe and the way it works is very simple and uncomplicated: Like attracts like.

The perfect frosting for your cake is out there, but it will not appear until your cake is ready!

So, now I've learned and I'm sharing the secret with you. Only when the time is right will I find the person who can love me at the same time I love him. Together we will find that place in each other that knows it's real. Until I am ready, that person will not appear. Until he is ready, he will not find me. In the meantime, I will not settle for a false or temporary version of what I want. I will wait for the right flavor.

Taking Control

So my decision to fly solo for one year was made and by doing so, I have been more peaceful than ever because I know without doubt, it is the right thing to do. By allowing myself to love myself fully and trust God, I am at peace and know that I am now closer than ever to attracting my perfect frosting.

He's closer than I even know.

For more information, I have listed some valuable books and resources at the end of this book for your further study and en-lightenment. I encourage you to let this book be the beginning of your journey, not the end of it.

A man is what he thinks about all day long.
~Ralph Waldo Emerson

An Affirmation for Attracting
the Good Stuff into Your Life:

I am open to the blessings that are lined up for me.
I allow all that is good to enter my life.

Exercise #7:

Think about the times throughout each day that you say something negative whether about someone else, or about yourself. For one week, note each incident where you engaged in gossip or made a negative comment. Even write down when you had a negative thought! I'm sure, just like me you will shock yourself with how habitual and commonplace negativity has become in your life whether at home or work. As you bring these ideas into your awareness, make a conscious effort to replace those thoughts and words with positive and uplifting statements.

*NOTES:

I cannot give you the formula for success, but I can give you the formula for failure--which is:
Try to please everybody.
~Herbert Bayard Swope

Beef Cake

Some Tough Love for
the Man in Your Life

*T*his chapter is for the man in your life. If he won't read the whole book, (even though you asked sweetly, right?) do whatever it takes to get him to read this chapter. Men sometimes find themselves with a partner who probably has felt like me at some point or another. Men also have a whole different set of issues because they too have been programmed in certain ways by their upbringing or experiences.

They may have been raised by a mom who waited on them hand and foot, spoiled them rotten, and left you to deal with the results. Or their experiences with women may have been disappointing, even heartbreaking. Only you can decide whether or not he's worth hanging in there for the long haul and only he can decide if he wants to love you.

Guys, if you haven't already done so, I encourage you to at least turn back and read the chapter on the Law of Attraction. If you have ignored the law, it's time to fess up, man up, and set things on the right path.

It's been said that "Men are from Mars and Women are from Venus." In my mind, men all too often choose their cake with little thought to anything but immediate gratification. A quick grab-and-go snack mentality that sometimes turns into a satisfying meal. More often, it doesn't.

As a man, if you've ever wondered what makes women tick (although I have to add here that all women are not made from the same mold; they are as unique as snowflakes) why you keep attracting the women you do, and why we walk out; this book may help you.

Let's see if you recognize yourself in this roster of bad boys:

1. The Mama's Boy

Nobody does things, bakes, or cooks like Mama. Maybe you still live in the basement? She does your laundry? Convenient, I know, but lame. Stop being a boy. Grow up and be a man. You don't need to go from Mama's kitchen to your mate's kitchen with no time on your own figuring out how to be self-sufficient and strong. There is also something to be said for being overly critical as well. You can't criticize someone into being perfect and when you find one that is as close to ideal as you've ever seen, criticism just drives her away.

2. The Commitment-Phobe

I just know there is a tastier cupcake right around the next corner … If I commit to Sally, Mary Beth will appear and be a much more satisfying morsel of goodness. Stop! Get your own life/house in order, then let the Law of Attraction send you the ideal mate.

The yin to your yang. When you find her, nurture that relationship with all your heart. It's fine to appreciate other women, develop female friendships, admire businesswomen, but your ideal mate is the key to your lock. Even if you've been hurt before, it's time to make a commitment. Give it everything you've got. Half measures will get you half way.

3. Peter Pan Syndrome Sufferer

"I don't wanna grow up, I'm a Toys 'R Us kid ..." Remember that jingle? Is life just one big game to you? Or a series of play dates? If so, it's time to grow up. There are advantages to being an adult. The Bible tells us: When I was a child, I spoke and thought and reasoned as a child. But when I grew up, I put away childish things. A man who thinks and acts like a child will never attract a woman who is looking for a man to be her partner for life. She doesn't want to be your mommy, and you don't want her to be. Adult relationships are partnerships between equals, not mother and child.

4. The Playboy

Hugh Hefner wannabes, this is for you. Are you convinced that quantity beats quality? Here's some food for thought: Hugh Hefner was recently engaged to be married. Again. But his bride became a runaway bride because even though he may choose marriage, his life is anything but monogamous. Looks are great, but fleeting, and sitting alone in your hot bachelor pad will one day get very old. One delicious cake beats an armful of tasteless snacks every time.

5. The Long-suffering Sad Sack Victim

She wrecked my pickup truck, kicked my dog, and broke my danged ol' heart. Aw, poor baby. Breaking up is tough, no doubt about it. No one likes rejection, and that's what a breakup is. It changes how you view yourself and you can't help but you see yourself in your tormentor's eyes. Well, go ahead and cry a river, but then build a bridge and get over it. It's time to move on. Trust the universe. She wasn't the one for you. Miss Right is still out there and she's looking for you. Make yourself visible and available and she will find you when the time is right.

6. The Homosexual on the River of de Nile

"Honey, I love, love, love shopping for antiques, looking at decorating magazines, and painting your toenails, but making love to you is such a drag!" If this is you, do not try to fit the wrong key into the right lock. Be who you are. Do some serious soul-searching and figure out what you really want. Today there are unlimited options for partnerships and family structure.

Once upon a time, gay men would court, date, and marry women so they could have a 'normal' family life complete with children and this is still happening today. Often they did it for career reasons or because they had religious families who would never understand. By indulging yourself in this charade, you harm the woman who thought you were going to be the beef-cake of her dreams, and you really harm any children that come into your sham of a marriage. Be honest, be who you are, don't break someone's heart by pretending to be something you're not.

7. The Boss

"Honey, let's do things my way, or you're fired!" This macho-man knows it all. He is large and in charge. If this is you, you're not ready for a true partnership, the most fulfilling of all relationships. While most enlightened women really do want a man who is ready to accept his place as head of the household, she also wants to be treated as an equal partner and respected for her contribution to the home and relationship. Be a co-partner, not the boss, or you may find yourself fired rather than on fire with passion.

8. The Jock

Oh, the games boys do play! This guy is the cousin of Peter Pan and often doubles as a Mama's Boy. Is this you? Is The Game everything? If the game is turned on, you aren't. Women will leave this playa' in the locker room with his sweaty buds, at least until he decides to figure out some priorities. At some point, all those buddies will get married and move on and you'll be left humming a tune about the good old days with no one to care.

9. Casper the Absentee Ghost

This guy is hooked on fishing, addicted to golf, a workaholic, hunter, or any number of other pursuits that keep him missing in action. Female relationships come several spots down on his list of priorities. You may get lucky and find a woman who enjoys the same pursuits; this would be the Law of Attraction working overtime, but it can happen. If it doesn't, however, eventually your savvy gal is going to get tired of spending more time alone than a hibernating bear. She will either be sad and weepy, or she will become 'all one' instead of alone and you two will begin leading separate lives. This usually does not end well. No one wants to deny you the pursuit of a hobby, we all need them, but moderation is called for. Including your partner or at least acknowledging some 'couple' time is key.

10. The Add-Ick

If you have any inkling of an idea that you have a substance or alcohol abuse problem, seek help, not a mate! Until you are strong and healthy, you have no business pursuing a relationship. This is critically important if children are involved, either yours or hers. Women tend to be 'fixers' and are unfortunately often drawn to those who are broken or in need of care. No doubt someone is going to believe that in spite of your additions, she can 'make it all better.' I urge you to spare her and seek help from professionals. Only then will you be a good candidate for frosting.

11. The Caveman (a.k.a. Tarzan)

Do you call your mate demeaning names like 'chick,' 'broad,' 'babe,' et cetera? Is her 'proper place' in the kitchen or bedroom, never the boardroom? Do you refuse to date women who make more money than you do? Or are taller than you? Do you insist on always paying for everything, selecting where you'll go on dates, and be the guy who knows best about money, property, which car to buy, and all things 'manly'? There's one word for you: Ugh. Jane is not gonna like your Tarzan act, at least not for long.

12. The Leech

When you find someone you're crazy about (and 'crazy' is the operative word here), do you want to spend every minute of your life with her? You over-text, over-call, obsess, and resent every moment she spends with others. You are suspicious of co-workers, jealous of her family and friends, and secretly suspect that she's cheating on you. The underlying problem here is usually your own lack of self-confidence. There is nothing that will drive a woman away faster than an obsessive, jealous mate. She may be flattered in the beginning, but again, this will not end well. Be patient, work hard on baking your ideal life-cake, and wait for the Law of Attraction to send you the right partner and there will be no need for jealousy or obsession.

If you have noticed your partner looking sad or seeming to have a distant, faraway look in her eyes, you may be one of the dirty dozen. Don't start trying to figure out what's wrong by worrying about her. Look inward first. Examine the relationship as honestly and objectively as you can and see if what you're doing may be driving her away.

If you decide - after an exhaustive self-examination that it's not you, then she may feel incomplete and want to search for her own true self.

Girls, you aren't off the hook!

This chapter is for the man in your life, but it is not about pointing out all their flaws. As many issues as I've listed above for men, women have just as many if not more. How many women do you know that are so attached to their mother that there is really no room for a healthy relationship with any man? And this is just one example.

Every single type of man I've listed has a female counterpart from the Jock to the Leech! So I'm not picking on men. But there is one other issue that every woman experiences and every man in a relationship with that woman has to deal with: **Hormones**.

There I said it, the 'H' word. Almost every time you say the word these days, women just roll their eyes like it's an overblown complaint from the men in their lives, but you know what? It's not overblown. It exists and as much as we'd like to think that we have it all under control, we don't.

Hormones are chemicals that run through our bodies. Sometimes they rage, sometimes they just exist unnoticed, but they have the power to turn a sweet, happy women into something from a scene in The Exorcist. How many times, during a certain week of the month have you bitten off your partner's head for squeezing the toothpaste wrong, looking at your wrong, or just because he breathes? And don't think the men don't notice or are unaware of what is going on. They know what week each month to either avoid you or walk on eggshells. You may deny the effect of hormones all you want but it doesn't make it any less real or less damaging to your relationships.

Being aware of the issue is the first step just like in every other area you want to change. When you know your emotions are a little ragged due to a surge in estrogen, force yourself to acknowledge it. Take a deep breath before you say anything and if at all possible, avoid confrontations during this time. It does no good for a simple discussion on what to have for dinner to dissolve into a weepy mess.

Of course, with age comes menopause and this issue is heightened because the hormones can rage for years. This is the time that you should consider getting your hormone levels checked. There are many therapies, both holistic and pharmaceutical, that can tame the beast and allow you some relief (and your partner too!). There are a lot of marriages that dissolve right about the time the woman hits menopause and it certainly has the potential to aggravate and heighten any issues in the relationship that already exist.

I can't help but feel a little sorry for the guys on this front. They have no idea what it's like to have hormones take over your emotions, but they also have no way to help fix it. They are completely helpless and after a few months (or years) of being told they can't do one thing right it can be hard to feel any kind emotions toward the woman they are with. We all hear the jokes about how overly demanding women can be and the thing is, it's really true. Every women has to acknowledge the fact that hormones do have an effect on their state of mind and take control – and responsibility – for their words and actions.

There is no failed relationship that is one hundred percent the fault of one partner. We all must know that any issues or baggage we bring to the mix must be dealt with in a positive manner, and any ongoing issues acknowledged. You can't expect your partner to be perfect, but you can expect that they take responsibility for their own problems and either work on them, or allow them to be a deal breaker.

You have to do your own growing,
No matter how tall your grandfather was.
Abraham Lincoln

An Affirmation for Being a
Complete person
(man or woman!)

I take 100% responsibility for my behaviors and actions.
I choose how I react to every event and I choose peace,
serenity and happiness.

Exercise #8:

Look at the various types of people(men) I listed. What elements of those personas do you have? Write them down. Take responsibility for the areas that might be straining your relationship and commit to working on you. You can never force someone else to work on their problems but you can work on you Don't wait. Start now to be the happiest version of you possible.

Now think back to some occasions when you and your spouse got into ridiculous arguments. Do you notice or acknowledge that there could be some chemicals (hormones) making things worse? If so, make an appointment with your doctor or seek advice for holistic solutions to keep those hormones at bay.

So do not fear, for I am with you;
do not be dismayed, for I am your God.
I will strengthen you and help you;
I will uphold you with my righteous
right hand.
Isaiah 41:10

Devil's Food Cake

When Things Go Bad

• •

Y ou chose your partner, your wedding cake, and your life's direction with great care, but it all falls apart. The crumbly pieces land everywhere for you and others to clean up. It's a mess. The recipe has failed. Perhaps it was your fault. You forgot to add eggs, you put in too much sugar or not enough spice. The oven was too hot or too cold. Whatever the reason, it's now clearly a disaster.

Sadly, many women I know who are married hate their lives and have no clue how to manage it. More often than not, they got married for all the wrong reasons:

* *Family pressure*
* *The desire not to be left behind when friends are all getting married*
* *The uniquely female attraction to all things 'wedding' involved*
* *The desire for children (noble, but it only works when you marry a good father figure)*

* *A strong physical attraction to a man - passion*
* *A desire for constant companionship (a live-in buddy and helpmate)*
* *A desire for financial stability and security*
* *A need for physical security (perhaps in a desperate flee from*
  an abusive home-life)

The justifications for a poorly thought-out marriage are endless. Women innately crave marriage or that long term committed relationship. It's as old as humanity and as undeniable as the pull of gravity. The worst terror women have is being old and alone. Our ancestors had the need for a protector and provider hardwired into their brains, but the world has changed and so must we to shake these old genetic impulses. Even today, when women think of being that iconic 'spinster' or 'old maid' it can lead to a desperate mate search. Any port in a storm we think. Any man is better than no man. That is the stereotypical thinking that has plagued women for generations. We must free ourselves from those shackles and tired old paradigms.

Women have even subjected themselves to arranged marriages or 'shot gun' weddings forced on them by over-protective relatives. Pregnancy is often the catalyst, but fortunately in today's western world women have more options than those poor sisters of past eras or that still suffer in more closed societies. We get to choose now, but still many women give in to the pressures of old. Many first marriages are based upon unsound reasoning. Second and third marriages tend to be more happiness focused and result from a better selection process. The recipe has been refined, but it still may not be perfect yet.

I have been there, so I understand the fear of being alone that grips us, however once the seed of desire is planted for true happiness, there's no turning back. The wheels of motion take over and, depending on how great the wish, will determine the speed in which the prize is achieved. Many women tread water in their daily married lives, never floating on their backs looking at the sun, never swimming full bore toward the Island of True Happiness. They merely exist, but that need not be. I urge you to seek real happiness, and that comes from inside you. Once you get the internal happiness barometer on track the external will become much clearer.

Divorce or Diverse?

Divorce is a frightening word that can be so scary it creates what I call 'trapped' feelings. We are afraid of going it alone, but are also desperately unhappy. It is my belief, however, that no one should feel as if they live in a cage or prison with no possibility of parole. There are ways to make the best of the situation (unless, of course, abuse is involved, which cannot be tolerated.) and even improve the marriage. When we hear the word divorce, the famous country song from the 60's that spelled the word out comes to mind and I lived through many parental divorces. Yes, divorces, plural, so I know what I am talking about. When divorce happens to a child, it can be very frightening, even after multiple divorces. In fact, the more it happens, the scarier it is, because it feels as though you're on swinging bridge with no stability in sight. But I'm also here to tell you that you can survive. With a little insight, you can even thrive, but sometimes it takes a while.

We can find ourselves in situations that seem helpless and hopeless, like we have no control. Excuses arise and fear is the dominating factor. An unhealthy marriage is just that, unhealthy for all involved, including the children. A good marriage must act as potting soil for growing healthy children, not an acid bath that destroys joy and self-esteem.

I am no marriage counselor, but I have had more than my share of good times and bad both in my own relationships and through witnessing those of parents, friends, and family. One member of my family has been married nine times, so I have seen firsthand the strong drive and desire to find mister right. No one recipe for happiness is perfect for everyone. We must each determine what we want our cake to taste like and look like. Every situation is different and how you choose to find your bliss is specifically designed for you because you are the creator of it. It is my intention to encourage individual happiness in everyone and show how that can lead to a strong and healthy relationship. How one goes about obtaining this is a personal decision, and one I cannot direct, it must come from you. My intention is only to inspire and encourage the journey. Perhaps nudge you into the kitchen to design that ideal recipe. Study what it is exactly that you want, and then go about the business of getting it.

We have only moments here on Earth when you look at the span of human existence. Moments I have found to be so precious, I wish to live in calm everlasting peace. Peace, just like everything else I talk about, boils down to one thing: What do you really want? To achieve bliss, you must decide.

Recently, I was chatting with a friend I have known for many years. We have not seen each other in a very long time, but we found each other on Facebook and rekindled our beautiful friendship. Eventually we met for a long lunch and got around to talking about life, love, and happiness. I saw deep sadness in her eyes as she looked like I used to look when I longed for completeness.

"Are you happy in your marriage?" I asked her, and the answer was, of course, no. Then I asked why she was choosing to stay. She seemed surprised that I phrased the question as a choice because clearly she acted as though there was no choice in the matter.

Her answer was similar to all the excuses I have heard before and ones I had also used myself:

"I really don't have a choice. We have such an established life and I love my house. Plus, I don't want to hurt him. He's not a bad guy."

Bad guy. Bad recipe. We assign the ideas of 'good' or 'bad' to a situation when the truth is that they are just not right for us. It has nothing to do with who they are as a person. A relationship is about how you are together. It was as if all those years ago, she panicked when she was in the marriage bakery and quickly chose plain pound cake, but her heart yearned for the luscious red velvet with fudge frosting.

My next question was:

"So, you are choosing a house and the security it offers over real happiness?"

By not acting she was, in fact, making a choice:

No decision is a decision.

I was very straightforward, so it took her a while to answer. She said she had never thought of it like that and then her wheels began to spin and her desire for happiness bubbled to the surface. She wanted that red velvet cake. Now she is taking charge of her life for the first time and I see the strength, courage, and determination of an independent woman growing daily. She has gone back to work and is developing her recipe. She will no doubt be back in the bakery before long, knowing that her options are wide open and she need not limit herself or deny herself the joy of true bliss. My intent isn't to break up marriages, but to save both partners from a loveless relationship. It does neither the man nor woman any good to be unhappy and when two people choose to part, they are also choosing to imagine another life for themselves and a chance at real happiness. That is brave and courageous.

If there's a glimmer of love left in a relationship and both parties are committed to working it out, I believe a marriage can recover. Sometimes, however, it's best to move forward and not waste time trying to kick the dead horse back to life because of guilt, fear of hurting the other person, or what will the family think, oh, and the kids. How many times have I heard:

"We must stay together for the kids."

As a child experiencing my parents' failed marriages several times, I would much rather my parents find happiness with another than to see them constantly arguing, cheating, or abruptly leaving the other after a fight. It is turmoil that causes childhood insecurity, not the changing of a spouse. This may not be the case in all unhealthy relationships, but when love is missing, everyone can feel it. Everyone.

Staying for the wrong reasons is not fair to anyone. No matter what has happened between the two parties, each partner deserves a shot at their own happiness. Staying for the wrong reason is detrimental to the mind, and therefore to your life. Remember, what our heartfelt vibrations emit, so shall we attract a matching vibration into our lives. It is not selfish to desire happiness. In fact, if you are unhappy in your marriage, chances are great that your spouse and your children are not happy either. How could they be? So, in a nutshell, find a way to be happy, and then keep doing that.

Don't marry the person you think
you can live with; marry only the
individual you think you can't live without.
~Dr. James C. Dobson

An Affirmation for Turning a Bad Recipe
into a Generous Helping of Joy

*Today I allow myself to love those in my life uncondi-
tionally. By doing this, I am at the highest vibration and
attract the same back to me.*

Exercise #9:

Think about the relationship you are currently in (if
any). Does it fill you with dread or warmth? Only you can
decide if you want to make a go of it, or if it will be better
to make a clean break. Write down your concerns. Now
look at what you wrote. Are these reasons or excuses?
Nothing can outweigh your personal happiness or is more
important. Make a plan to improve or increase your own
happiness by loving yourself unconditionally.

*NOTES:

When one door of happiness closes,
another opens; but often we look
so long at the closed door that we
do not see the one which has been
opened for us.
~Helen Keller

Wedding Cake

How to Know if it's
Time for Some Frosting

*O*nly when you are living your happiest, healthiest, most blissful life, and you stand firmly in your own space with your feet on firm soil should you consider adding frosting to you cake life.

When I first started learning about the laws of the universe and how we play a role in the whole cosmos, I was learning about deliberate creation. That includes manifesting desires, living abundantly, prayer, meditation, allowing and many other concepts. I wanted to know more and became a sponge cake, soaking up what I was learning.

Let Go and Let God

My Christian upbringing had me questioning so many things that I wanted confirmation that this was in line with the teachings of Christ. I felt it in the core of my being, however there was that underlying thought that I needed to know how this knowledge relates to Christianity. I was seeking the answers and heard one of the teachers who appeared in the hit movie, The Secret, was a professed Christian and also very much a teacher of the Law of Attraction. I pursued making contact with this person.

My question sounded something like:

*"I heard you are a Christian and I was wondering
how all of this relates to Christianity?"*

The reply I received:

*"Think about that question and ask yourself,
why do you care what I believe?"*

I sat there for a moment and asked myself:

"Why do I care what he believes?"

After all, this person and what he believes has nothing to do with me and what I believe. He is not even someone in my life, so what difference did his belief system matter to me?

I realized what each of us believes is very personal and has nothing to do with alignment with any sort of dogma or with the 'rules' of organized religion. There is no one on Earth who knows more about my personal journey than I do. I would ever allow any one to force their opinions or views on me in hopes that I was following the 'right' path to heaven.

I possess the inner guidance system that is designed to lead each of us to our own destiny. That GPS chip is in our God-given genetic recipe. We only need to tune in to it and follow the pathway it shows us.

The peace that overcame me at that moment of revelation was indescribable, that the magnificence within is bestowed in each and every one of us and we all have the ability to do great things while here. Joy, happiness, and love are within our reach and placed along our pathway for us to discover.

Choosing Frosting for our Cake

As you make your way through your own journey, you may work on your career, your finances and other areas of your life as you go. Some will be hard, others much easier but growth in all areas will give you a wonderful sense of accomplishment and peace. At some point, though, you will want more.

So now your life cake is coming together nicely you are liking its flavor and texture. You decide you'd like to add a little relationship frosting to your life. "It's time," you tell yourself. Then you have second thoughts and you ask yourself, "Why is this step even necessary?" Then you realize even some of the sweetest cakes taste a little better when topped with the right flavor of frosting.

Once you start thinking of a life partner as an enhancement, and not a necessity or requirement, it puts you in a very emotionally healthy space to attract the right kind of person that is also in a great healthy space.

How to select the right flavor...

My first piece of advice is:

Avoid the **Dirty Dozen** frosting types from Chapter 8.

My second piece of advice is:

Don't go searching for it! If you feel like your cake needs some frosting, be open to finding the right flavor. But to go out in search of it, will yield no good results. This is in reference to 'muscling the universe.'

The sweetest experiences in life are those that 'just happen' to us. We remember those as special moments and they can create everlasting flavor for many years to come. Of course, we know they don't just happen, but when we set our intention it can still take us by surprise when it manifests and that perfect person appears in the most unlikely place – like in line at the grocery store or sitting at the next table in a restaurant. The truth is that person has always been there but you didn't notice because you weren't ready and neither was he.

The saying, *"Let Go & Let God"* comes to mind when pondering this particular topic because it is all about allowing things to come to you, rather than forcing your will on them. I have found the harder we search for something, the harder it is to find. Give up on the quest and decide to allow life to unfold at the right time for you. I recently gave up looking for Mr. Right. All I kept finding was Mr. Right Now So, I decided it was time to just let my life evolve without searching. I spent several months in the state of allowing, wondering if I would ever find him. After all, FedEx was not going to ring my doorbell with the perfect package, all neatly wrapped up and ready for marriage. (Wouldn't that be cool, though, huh?)

Remember, once your cake is done, if you are attracted to another, chances are they are a decent person and if not a lover, could be a good 'friend' ingredient, regardless of whether or not anything else develops. Always keep in mind, friend first, then lover maybe. Friends are a vital part of the overall ingredient list of your life cake and can make the internal ingredients come together even better. Just because there may not be a love connection, if they are sweet...keep 'em around. Goodness spawns goodness. The more the better, the sweeter the batter.

Chemistry, Sex Appeal

Okay I will admit that on occasion I will meet someone that is so hot and awesome, I'd love to make him mine right then and there! Those are my hormones talking and I know it, but we all have the experience of meeting someone and all of the ingredients seem to be perfect. He even reminds you of the best frosting you ever tasted! But, is he really the one? Chances are, he's not, but he could be. Get to know him. See how well his ingredients are mixed in his cake and see if your flavors complement each other.

When the frosting comes with extras - like the sprinkles you loved as a kid - he is darn near irresistible. Perhaps his sprinkles include the ability to dance like Fred Astaire, charm your mother, do magic tricks, or maybe his politics line up perfectly with yours. Those unexpected but adorable little extras are fun and make you want to devour him. Caution: Those sprinkles may just be quickly-dissolving pure colored sugar with no nutritional value and no real substance, so take your time!

You might get the dissatisfaction of wanting more and more until you've lost control of the situation and find yourself wondering "why am I feeling so hungry and craving this stuff?" We tend to lose ourselves quickly once we feel the addictive force of lust/ love. Keep your head clear and stay in control of you. Once you feel the 'need' for this flavor, you have to back up a bit and examine your ingredients again. What is your cake lacking that is requiring this substitute? You will discover it, then you can move on or move forward, whichever is appropriate.

You have all the time in the world and relationships are not on any sort of deadline except for those we impose on them. There is no rule that says you have to date for X amount of time and then you have to 'move it to the next level'. You can take as long as you want and should do what is right for you no matter what anyone else thinks.

I have some friends that a number of years ago both divorced. They had each been in possessive, dysfunctional marriages and had no desire whatsoever to be married again. These two met and on one of their first dates made an agreement that neither of them would ever even mention the 'M' word (marriage). It worked! Their agreement gave them freedom from the pressure of wondering where the relationship was going. They dated happily for four and a half years while they each worked on their own issues. Finally, they agreed that they were ready and married in their swimsuits on a beach in the Bahamas. They have now been married more than 13 years.

You deserve your own happy ending and by focusing on your own personal growth and happiness it will come to be – when the time is right.

Here Comes the Bride or Bridle?

Be careful not to apply your frosting too early or too much at once. This can ruin the overall taste and appearance of your life cake, not to mention any chances of removing it without having to remake part of the cake. Proceed with caution. You have worked hard to bake your sweet life cake. The last thing you want to do is ruin it with the wrong frosting or slap it on too soon. What happens when you try to frost a warm cake? It melts into a big hot mess and that's what can happen if you rush out with your new found sense of self worth. It can get lost again very easily because it hasn't had time to become a natural part of who you are. There is no rush. Give yourself time to cool.

Already Married?

If you are already married and in a loving relationship and you want to save your marriage, you can remake your cake with husband frosting as a bonus. The trick is open and honest communication with your spouse. He needs to know and understand that you are remaking your life, not his, and that your ultimate goal is a stronger marriage – not to get rid of him. As we've discussed, many men will react in an insecure manner to big changes, from a new hairdo to a new career, and it will be up to you to reassure him. Be open about what you need from him and what your goals are. Don't expect him to placidly readjust all his expectations or change his daily routines to accommodate your new yoga classes, jogging, career goals, or style of clothing.

The new you will take some time to get used to for both you and him. Changes are best introduced incrementally with tact, subtlety, caring, thoughtfulness, and intelligence. Contrary to pop-culture thought processes and propaganda, men and women are different creatures. We experience things from very different perspectives and you'll need to ensure that he is strong enough to handle the new and improved version of you. Tease and taunt him with the promise of how good your new cake is going to taste and he'll probably enjoy the changes so much he'll help!

Not becoming a pull-apart Cake

How can you remain whole when your husband, kids, employer, clients, pets, and even loyal girlfriends want a piece of you? You feel pulled and twisted, this way and that, and there's never enough time for yourself. Life can be out of control with soccer games, recitals, homework, entertaining, vet visits, and many other 'have to dos' all getting in the way of your me time. As women, we tend to be self-sacrificing, always letting others' needs come first, even when we are unhappy about it. Feeling frustrated when you don't get your time and guilty when you do. What's a girl to do?

Your goal is to have it all, not do it all!

Three words: Organize. Prioritize. Delegate.

Let's take them in order.

1. Organize:

You can never be your best self, let alone bake a great sweet life cake, without some organization. There are many books and websites devoted to ways to get organized, from closet design companies to professional for-hire organizers and folks who will set up your home office, so I won't waste a lot of time with specifics here. It is critical that you do it, however. You cannot think and make logical decisions when you're in the midst of chaos and clutter. You will never function well with missing ingredients, lost keys, mismatched socks, stained clothing, or when in need of a haircut. Make a list of the places in your life that need to be cleaned out and organized, and then tackle them one at a time. Toss out, donate, store, and designate a place for everything. This goes for your closet, office/desk, car, garage, kitchen – every aspect of your life. You will be amazed at how good you will feel, and how much more you will be able to accomplish in a day once everything is well organized. No more time wasted hunting for things, no more paying for things twice because you can't find them, no more re-printing documents or information because they are lost in the slush pile euphemistically called your inbox.

One other aspect of organization should include a filing system and a way to keep track of expenses for tax filing purposes. Learn to get receipts for everything and file them away immediately. Your accountant will thank you and your refund or lowered tax rate will be enhanced as a result.

2. Prioritize:

What is most important? What is not so important? Start with a list of the things you spend (or would like to spend) your time on each week. Now break them down into seven days. For example, you take your children to school five days a week, go to yoga class (or want to) twice a week, get a massage once a week, go on a date with your husband one night a week, and any other important events that take place during your week. Try to make the list as comprehensive as possible. Some things may get lopped off later, some may be added, but this gives you a starting point. Some things are critical and non-negotiable, others are voluntary or optional. You do not have to get a latte every morning; you do have to do your taxes once a year. In creating a schedule, even a tentative one, always leave room for what makes you happy and for those things that invariably pop up and say, "Boo!"

3. Delegate:

You do not have to do everything on that list yourself. In fact, if you have children, they will benefit from helping you with chores.

It will make them self-sufficient and capable. No kids? Not to worry. Your mate, (if you have one) is more capable than you give him credit for. And if he's not, he should be. Don't try to carry the burden alone, doing so only engenders bitterness and resentment. On behalf of the man in your life, I will tell you that you'll need to let go a bit of the controls. Let him do it his way. It may not be your way (probably won't be) but it'll get done. Don't criticize, just be grateful for the help and let it go. Another alternative is to pay someone to do those things that must be done, but don't enhance your life. If you love gardening and yard work, go for it. If not, pay someone and save your nails. Even hiring a professional organizer to get you on the right path is often a worthwhile investment in your sanity.

A word here to stay-at-home moms:

You and your children will both benefit from at least one day a week apart. Put your child in a great day care, or trade 'free days' with another mom so that you each get a day to be alone, to perhaps enjoy a bubble bath and a good book. Your child will have a great time and so will you!

> *The more grateful you are for everything good*
> *that comes into your life, the more closely you*
> *place your mind in contact with that power in life*
> *that can produce greater good.*
> *~ Christian D. Larson*

An Affirmation for Finding
the Love of your Life

I am in a state of allowing. Allowing the desires of my heart to manifest to me the love of my life. The one who is my one for all time, my equal, my partner.

Exercise #10:

If you want to find a great love, it is important to define exactly what you want. Make a list of the attributes that you would like this person to have. This will allow you to know when he shows up and also give you a way to keep yourself from getting involved with someone you have already decided isn't what you want.

If you are married, make a list of the things you want more of in your marriage. It might be things like communication, time together or sex. You decide and then once those things are put out into the universe as your desire you will start to make the decisions to make them happen.

*NOTES:

For God did not give us the spirit of timidity, but a spirit of power, of love, and of self-discipline."
~ 2 Timothy 1:7 (NIV)

Final Crumbs of Wisdom

Food for Thought

I would like to leave you with some final morsels from my 'Blissful Life Bakery'. From the beginning this journey, my personal fortunes are on the rise and I anticipate my perfect frosting to appear when the time is right. That said, I am taking things slowly and cautiously, enjoying each day as I find it, and not projecting too far into the future.

Individual Pathways

If you are ready to take the next step in your Life's journey, I recommend reading the teachings of others who live by this knowledge. I found myself craving any and all spiritual teachings I could get my hands on. I have placed at the back of this book a list of resources that have, and still do assist me with my walk. I mention my favorite authors and teachers who wish to raise the awareness level of the planet's inhabitants.

I Woke Up...Will You?

I woke up – not, of course, physically as if from a long nap, but spiritually and emotionally. I gained insight, to the possibilities in my life and all that I could accomplish. My awakening and the power of my conscience decision to finally go for my heart's desires will hopefully inspire you to join me.

Keep in mind, what I am sharing with you is strictly my perspective on what I learn daily by living with spiritual awareness. It is my hope that I inspire you while you are on your individual path. Remember, there are no right or wrong answers here, it's just my version of a Universal Law that governs us all. It is up to you to find your own translation of the message and experience the true joy which we all can have the privilege of experiencing. Design your life the way you wish. It really is up to us how we put this all together.

Nobody else is responsible for you. Your walk is your walk. Your ideas and ability to choose are all yours, nobody else's. In other words, bake your specially designed cake, just the way you like it. The purpose of this book is to set you on that path to self-discovery and self-fulfillment and it is my dream that you find yourself very soon happier, healthier, and enjoying the sweet life.

Friendly Advice or Control issue?

Straightforward advice, no matter how kindly it's offered, is usually unwelcome. Notice the body language of anyone to whom you are directing the unbidden advice and you will likely discover this to be true. I know for certain that I dislike any advice given to me, unless I specifically ask for it. Not sure why this is, however I see it as placing one's ideals and limitations on another.

So, if you are looking for me to tell you what to do...Sorry, I can only make decisions for myself. My intention is to empower, not to limit. I never give advice directly, however I am only too happy to discuss my theories and personal experiences. My ideas can be evaluated and understood without my actually giving advice on someone's specific situation. We are all on our own paths and what may be good for me, might not work for another. So, I elect to share what works for me and let my friends decide what works for them.

So, you ask:

"How will I know when I am a whole finished cake?"

First, let me reiterate that the journey toward wholeness is ongoing for our lifetime. What is whole today may only be a slice in some future existence, so personal and spiritual growth is something to be striven for daily.

You will know when you have achieved success, however, when you wake up daily with your custom designed routine that suits you and only you. Regardless of anyone or anything going on, you have a spring in your step and a song in your heart without the presence of another being the basis of your happiness. When you can feel good on your own, you've mastered your life.

Taking a Break

Like attracts Like. I recognized as long as I was incomplete, I would forever attract the same into my life as far as my partner. It was that realization that helped me decide to take a much needed break from the opposite sex so that I would really define and get clear about who I am as a person and what I truly want for my life.

I had decided after my bout with 'alone' all the way to becoming 'All One,' I did eventually want a man to share my life. The recipe for him, however, was not exactly clear to me. I still had so many things I needed and wanted to learn.

And Then There was Light

One day I woke up feeling empowered. I felt so alive! I was eleven months into my journey of the 'no relationship rule' and it suddenly felt different! Was I finally complete? I finally felt desirable and happy in my own skin.

I realized, no matter how long it would take, I was going to wait for my perfect frosting. Not to search, but to wait and allow my perfect partner to be guided to me.

I am now 2 years into my "all one" journey. I did try dating a very wonderful man for a few months, however soon discovered neither of our cakes were ready for frosting. We both made the decision to continue our journeys alone like two ships charting different paths - to eventually be whole enough to one day attract our perfect partners. I am so grateful we both realized this early enough to spare future heartaches; adult decisions that empowered us both to our individual wholeness.

Many of us struggle with the same issues. The same beliefs and fears that keep us down and drowning in a sea of disappointment, depression, sadness, fear and hopelessness take hold because our lives seem to be going nowhere. We are all spiritual beings and because of this, what we seek, our guides will lead us to. Whether it be a better job, better body, a loving husband, improved relationships or any of the other things we desire. Whatever it is you wish, you can have it all. Our energies are drawn from other humans unless we tap into God's pure source of energy by renewing ourselves on a consistent basis. When we make this personal time to connect and renew ourselves, the need for control and expectations is eliminated and we live in peace. Now it's your turn!

Dream Big

I will always dream big, no matter what. I never want to limit myself by only trying for what is probable, I want what is possible! I hope you will dream big too. Maybe it's a Texas thing – we do everything big in Texas!

As my life has evolved, I discovered there are always greater blessings waiting to be revealed. I must take each life experience and enjoy it so I can keep them coming and I'm finding my happiness keeps growing and growing. I wake every morning with the question, "Okay, God, which heart's desire am I going to experience today?"

Can you Spare Some Change?

Change is great, but only if it happens for the right reasons. In my opinion, trying to change in order to please another is never a good idea. Yes, you can compromise on those daily things that couples must always negotiate (I'll wash, you dry; I'll drive, you navigate) and you can certainly change your mind (Okay, we'll go to the mountains for vacation instead of the beach.) What I'm talking about is changing who you are for someone else.

For example:

You're with a guy you're crazy about, but he wants a woman who jogs and loves kayaking. You hate jogging, so much that you'd rather take a sharp poke in the eye. But you do it anyway, lacing up your cross-trainers at five in the morning every day. to accompany him on his daily run. It starts your day off miserably, but the nights are worth it, right? **Wrong.**

Spending your Saturday paddling a kayak in icy water when you'd rather be doing almost anything else is wrong as well.

Be who you are. He should love you for the woman who enjoys yoga and ballroom dancing. Of course, you can agree to join him for an occasional run, but he should also be willing to go dancing without complaint. That's called compromise. But if you try to hide your true pleasures or change your ideology for someone else it will go against your very core and resentment soon follows. Then anger. Then coffee cups zinged at his head – you get the picture. You are who you are, and you are special and unique. Embrace your uniqueness and wait to find someone who does too!

Let go of the Past

Embrace Today &

Reach for the Future ...

The past is gone, the future is uncertain. The only thing we truly have is this moment. Things from the past only serve as barriers, like road blocks thrown up in the path toward the good life.

What this means for your love life is that to find true love and live your best Cake life, you have to let go of past hurts. If your hands and heart are full of injustices, hurtful slings and arrows like rejections, insults, infidelity, or out and out betrayal, you cannot grab hold of tomorrow's joys. This is another key to the success of allowing the Law of Attraction to rule your life: Be open and accepting of its gifts. They are definitely more perfect for you than anything you could conjure up on your own.

I'm sure you've heard the expression 'live in the moment' but let's think about it. What does that mean? It means being fully engaged in what's going on in front of you. It means not half listening to the person you're with while texting someone else under the table. It means not taking phone calls when you're with someone. And by someone, I don't just mean a date, I mean your friends, your children, your spouse or mate, or even your boss. It means looking them in the eye and listening and responding to what they're saying. Once you make a habit of this, you will be amazed at what you will hear and see and how it improves your relationships on every front.

It also means listening to the music as opposed to letting it just be background noise, losing yourself in the play or concert, or looking at the spectacular scenery instead of letting it just zip by in a blur. No camera image can really capture the beauty of nature, no matter what the ads say. Ever seen a picture of the Grand Canyon that can make you gasp? I rest my case. Don't spend another trip looking through a lens. *Be there.*

Recipe Tips from the Delicious Cake Life Channel
to Achieve a Blissful Life

1. Remove Negativity

Negative opinions, gossip, judgments, worrying about things that haven't happened, expecting the worst, poor me mentality, depression, blaming others – these are all examples of negativity. Avoid as much negativity as possible. Just drop it. Think positive and positive things will come into your life. I promise.

2. Add Acceptance

Try your best to accept everyone, whether you always agree with their choices or not. I'm not talking about criminals, but everyone has problems now and then, and even your best friend can forget your birthday, neglect to pay you back the money she borrowed, or lose your favorite sweater she borrowed. Let it go!

3. Add Love in Generous Measure

This is one ingredient you can never have too much of. Pour it on with reckless abandon. You will never overdo it. Stop worrying about what you get back, and give instead with no expectation of return.

4. Add a Pinch of Laughter

Laugh at someone's joke, or tell one yourself. Better yet, laugh just for the sake of laughter. There is nothing more melodious than the sound of laughter. Even the worst situations can benefit from a humorous approach. Remember the old Mary Tyler Moore Show episode at the clown's funeral? One person started to giggle, then it spread throughout the chapel and soon everyone was laughing hysterically? What better tribute to the clown?

5. Live. Laugh. Love. In any order!

Start right now, today, to have the life you so deserve and happiness – true happiness – will be yours for the rest of your life.

The significance of a man is not in what he attains
but in what he longs to attain.
~Kahlil Gibran

Personal Declaration

I hereby declare my intention to claim what is rightfully mine:

The Sweet Life

I fully understand that said Sweet Life is rightfully mine and available to me by simply making the decision to change my life. I have a burning desire to make it so.

Signed:_____

Date:_____

Ways to get there:

Being grateful

✳

Developing healthy friendships

✳ ✳

Reading books that resonate with you
and what you are wishing for

✳

Participating in activities that make
you feel at ease.

"Heaven never helps the man who will not act."
~Sophocles

Each of us is different and can find many different things that make us tick. You will discover different things about yourself on this journey. After all, it is a journey of Self Discovery.

My personal Cake Ingredients

I personally like to:

* Spend quality time with my children
* Meditate
* Attend church
* Cook from tasty recipes
* Work-out
* Organize my home
* Invent and create prototypes
* Decorate
* Write
* Daydream (visualize)
* Listen to music
* Nurture plants
* Mentor others

*****Recipe Journal *****

This is your personal space for notes, inspirations, ideas, and a place to record the daily gifts you will receive from the Universe. Be sure to take advantage of the space by writing down issues, problems, thoughts, challenges, or cake ingredients for your sweet life recipe that occur to you. Use this book as an ongoing journal of your growth.

You will see below that I have included some prompts from my own journey; these are merely tidbits to urge you along your path. This space is for the expression of your heart's desires and what happens as you seek the sweet life.

I want to be _____.

I feel inspired by _____.

My new life looks like _____.

People love to be near me because I exude_____.

If I died today,

I would like people to remember my _____.

Cake: Sherry Wilsher

_____

_____

_____

_____

_____

_____

_____

_____

_____

_____

_____

_____

_____

_____

_____

_____

_____

_____

_____

_____

_____

_____

_____

_____

_____

_____

_____

_____

_____

_____

_____

_____

*Whenever I have knocked, a door has
opened. Wherever I have wandered, a
path has appeared.
I have been helped, supported,
encouraged and nurtured by people of
all races, creeds, colors and dreams.*

~**Alice Walker,**
In Search of Our
Mother's Garden

Cake: Sherry Wilsher

Cake: Sherry Wilsher

_____

_____

_____

_____

_____

_____

_____

_____

_____

_____

_____

_____

_____

_____

_____

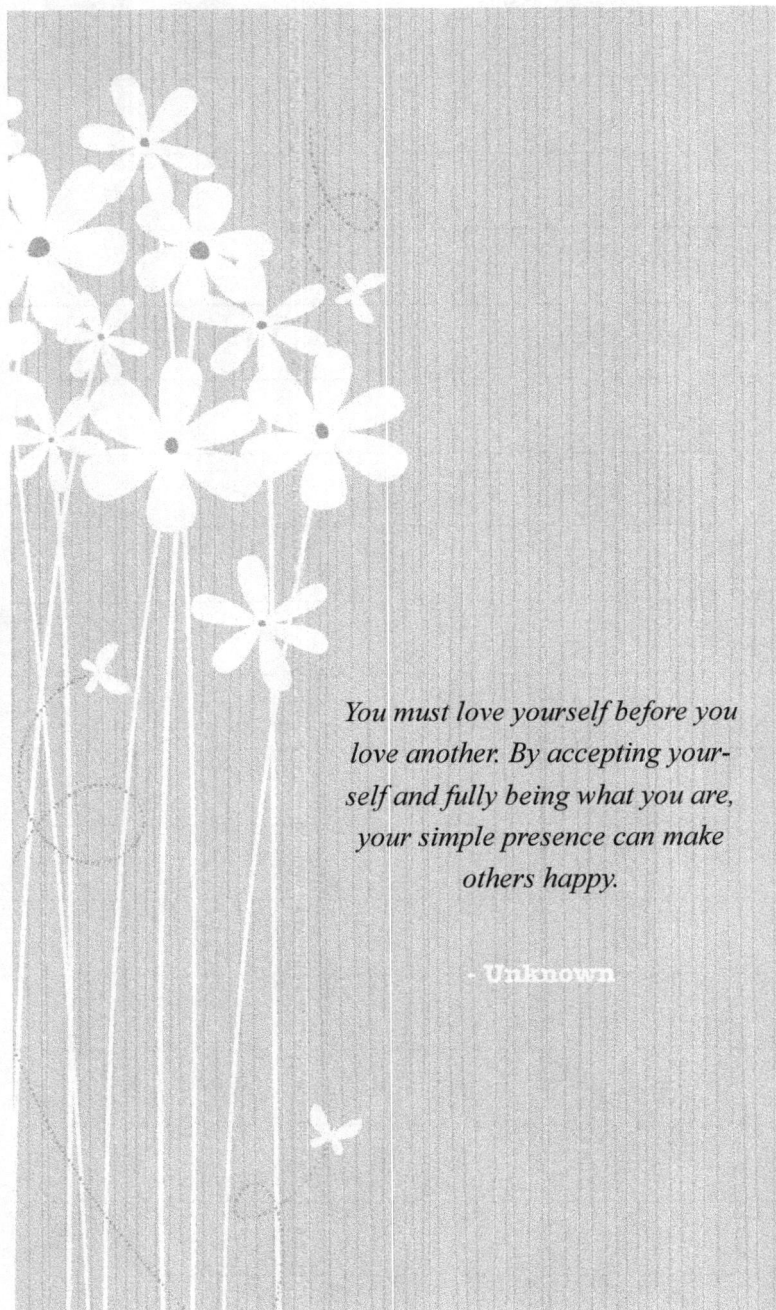

You must love yourself before you love another. By accepting your-self and fully being what you are, your simple presence can make others happy.

- Unknown

Cake: Sherry Wilsher

_____

_____

_____

_____

_____

_____

_____

_____

_____

_____

_____

_____

_____

_____

_____

_____

_____

_____

_____

_____

_____

_____

_____

_____

_____

_____

_____

_____

_____

_____

_____

_____

_____

_____

_____

_____

_____

_____

_____

_____

_____

_____

_____

_____

_____

_____

_____

As you become more clear about who you really are, you'll be better able to decide what is best for you - the first time around.

- Oprah Winfrey

Cake: Sherry Wilsher

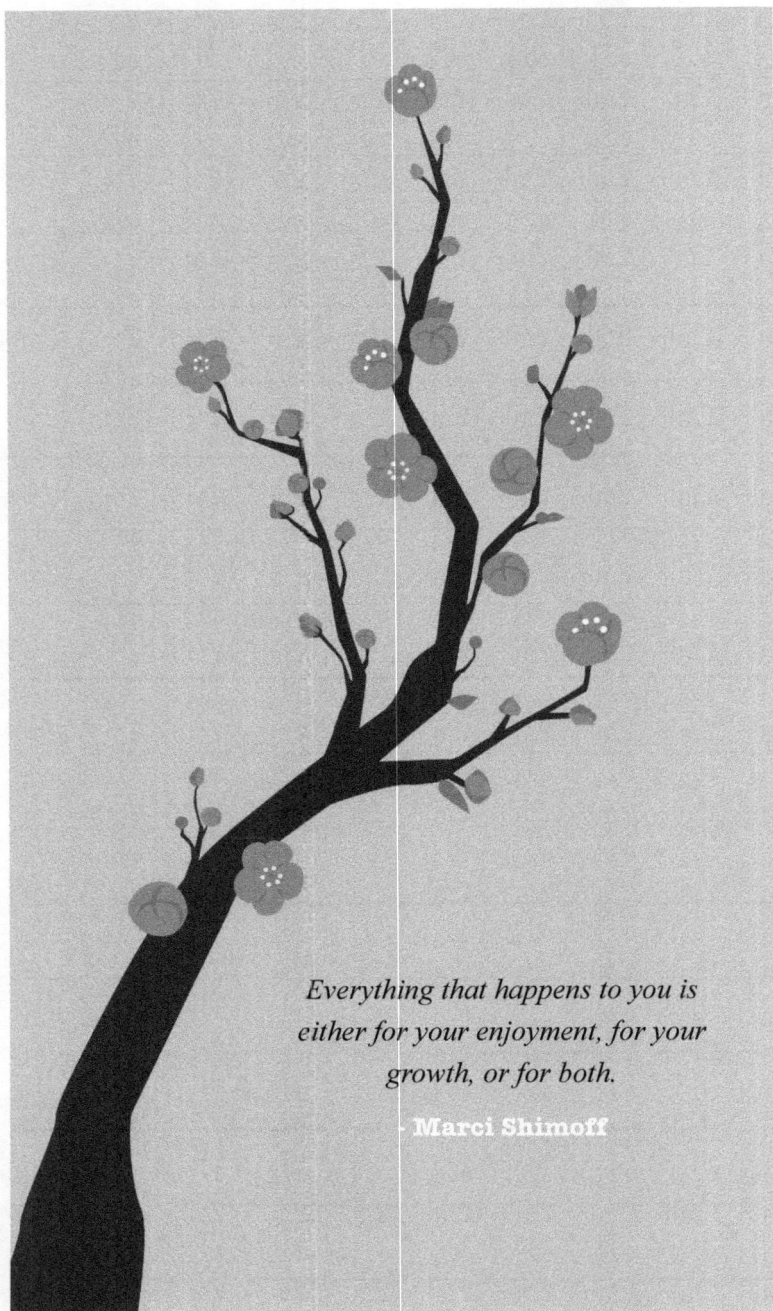

Everything that happens to you is either for your enjoyment, for your growth, or for both.

- Marci Shimoff

_____

_____

_____

_____

_____

_____

_____

_____

_____

_____

_____

_____

_____

_____

Cake: Sherry Wilsher

_____

_____

_____

_____

_____

_____

_____

_____

_____

_____

_____

_____

_____

*Acknowledgements**

There are so many people who have touched my life over the years. So many, in fact I could write a whole book with the stories I have regarding each person.

Thank you to all my beautiful friends and family. I appreciate your patience and inspiration while allowing me time to talk and dream about Cake for the past 3 years. Because you stood by me and believed in me while writing this book, you assisted with launching, yet another version of me.

"Sherry, The Author"…

Jacob Wilsher, my son – Thank you for inspiring me to be a better person by loving me regardless of my flaws and for being a main ingredient in my "Cake Life's recipe." Because of you, I live a more peaceful and balanced life. Also, thank you for assisting Ashlee in the MyCakeLife.com website. Your talents are much appreciated.

Ashlee Lynch – Thank you for being the creative soul that was able to take the dream from my mind and create such an amazing book cover, layout design, design for the *Cake Lifestyle* product line and MyCakeLife.com website. Your amazing creativity has allowed Cake to be an even sweeter experience. On a second note, thank you for being the daughter I never had. Because of you, I have been able to be a mom to a beautiful young lady. You are also a main ingredient to my "Cake Life Recipe."

566

Pat Barnhart – Thank you for your beautiful assistance during the "Recipe" designing process. Cake is even sweeter with you in the mix.

Dee Burks and Liz Ragland (Owners of TAG Publishing) – Thank you for your belief in me and Cake's message. It means so much to know people with your amazing talents in the publishing world recognized Cake as something of value. Because of this, I am truly grateful.

References & Resources

Suggested Reading for Feeding the Mind:

The Secret
Rhonda Byrne

The Success Principles
Jack Canfield

Happy for No Reason

&

Love for No Reason
Marci Shimoff

Change Your Thoughts, Change Your Life

&

Manifest Your Destiny
Dr. Wayne Dyer

You Can Heal Your Life
Louise Hay

Everyday a Friday
Joel Osteen

In the Mean Time
Iyanla Vanzant

Think and Grow Rich
Napoleon Hill

www.ingramcontent.com/pod-product-compliance
Lightning Source LLC
Chambersburg PA
CBHW031253090426
42742CB00007B/433